750 years of A Scottish School

RESPICE PROSPICE

AYR ACADEMY 1233-1983

John Strawhorn

ALLOWAY PUBLISHING, AYR.

FOREWORD BY
LORD ROSS OF MARNOCK

The people of Scotland are rightly proud of what is called the Scottish Tradition in Education. Perhaps 'traditions' would be more accurate. For that tradition is really a complex of principles, accepted and developed over the centuries leading to a national attitude to education; to the status of teachers; and the right to educational opportunity of each child.

It did not begin or end with John Knox's First Book of Discipline in 1560. His aim of a school in every parish took centuries to achieve. But it did point the way ahead. And there was fashioned early in Scotland a system of education, distinct from and in advance of other nations.

But three centuries before the Reformation and John Knox's proclamation, the Schule of Aire was already being linked immediately with the ancient Church of St. John. It was that school that became the Burgh grammar school and centuries later, in 1796, was re-designated Ayr Academy.

In the story of this one school over its 750 years of existence can be traced the whole histoy of Scottish education, from Church school to neighbourhood comprehensive. Ayr Academy is indeed unique. Of course during the centuries the Schule of Aire has been demolished and rebuilt over and over again — but never far from its original site, just west of the Sandgate.

The role of the school throughout the passing years has reflected the social changes in town and county. In my day it was still fee-paying in the primary with a selective intake from other schools in the town and the surrounding countryside at the age of twelve. At the end of the third year there was a further intake from Troon (Marr College was still on the drawing boards), Prestwick and Newton Park. We brought our old loyalties with us and to a certain extent never lost them. But the spirit of the Academy was such that we quickly became part of it.

At the Academy there was not just the earnest pressure towards learning. There was concern, helpfulness and enduring friendship. It is over fifty years since last I raced along Academy Lane to beat the deadline of Ned Loudon's bell, but my memories are still fresh and warm.

That Ayr Academy has survived all the upheavals of the ages is a tribute to generations of devoted teachers and the wisdom of many outstanding citizens to whom the well-being of the town of Ayr was linked with the continued existence and reputation of its ancient school. Ayr has other Academies today. But the old Schule of Aire lives on, sharing with them the modern challenge. If the past is anything to go by, Ayr Academy has still a long future.

William Ross

For its first 369 years, the school was at The Church of St. John.

In 1502 the 'instructor for the time being of grammatical studies in the burgh of Ayr' was Andrew McCormyll. In 1516 this post was held by John McKinneis. In 1519 Gavin Ross was appointed — by the town council — for one year, and in 1526 he was continued in this appointment for life. He was followed by Patrick Anderson (1541), Neil Orr (1547), William Nehary (1550), and John Buchan (1554).

This was still a church school, with classes meeting in the Church of St John, the teachers being chaplains of that church, and with Latin and Music as their subjects. But from 1519 onwards it was the town council of Ayr which was appointing the teachers and paying their salaries — initially 12 merks, later 20 merks a year, a merk being two thirds of a pound.

These masters were responsible for what was now principally a Latin or grammar school. Other persons were specialising on the musical side. In 1535 Robert Paterson was appointed to 'play the organ, sing in choir, and teach a sang schule.' In 1551 George Cochrane applied for a similar post. But clearly the school had become more secular in character, and with its two distinct departments was catering for a different clientele — the sons of burgh merchants, and lairds' sons from the landward area. That demand for schooling was growing is seen in 1550 when the town council noted that there were two private schools in Ayr. It ordered their teachers, Thomas Falconer and Thomas Spear, to hand over the fees they had collected; and prohibited all private schools in order to encourage attendance at the School of St John's. This policy they continued consistently for the next two hundred years, so securing a monopoly for the school they maintained.

Also in 1550 there is a brief glimpse of an occasion 'when the schule held not for the pest' and the routine of the school was interrupted by the plague. In 1556 we see the town council involving itself in what is now called curriculum development. It was decreed that pupils at the School of St John's 'be lairned by the Inglis and Latyne at the optioun and pleasure of the parents.' The teaching of English — reading and writing — was now a recognised separate subject, as well as Latin. Music had become of subsidiary importance. The School of St John's was in process of being converted into a burgh school.

THE TOWN COUNCIL TAKE CONTROL

When the Reformation came in 1560, a Protestant minister was appointed to the Church by Ayr town council. That council also took over entire responsibility for the school and its staffing. A new type of schoolmaster would replace the clergymen who had been in charge of schooling since 1233. The church school became the school at the church.

In 1559 the town council was complaining of 'the great hurt and misgovernance of the infants and bairns of this burgh this long time through not having an intelligent and qualified schoolmaster to teach them in manners and the art and science of the Latin tongue and grammar.' For some time there had been a rapid succession of different masters, a sufficient cause for concern. They therefore appointed John Or as master to give instruction to 'bairns of the town and to others repairing thereto.' As a protestant he could supply the appropriate religious instruction to provide them with 'manners', while 'the art and science of the Latin tongue and grammar' involved the teaching of reading and writing as a preliminary to the study of the classics. For most of the boys, a basic education would be all that their parents required. The occasional lad o' pairts would get the more advanced grounding in Latin necessary to take him on to university, and perhaps into the ministry.

The first former pupil of whom we have record belongs to this period. Robert Boyd of Trochrig (near Girvan) who was born in 1578 became a pupil at Ayr, as did his younger brother Thomas. Robert Boyd went on from Ayr burgh school to Edinburgh University, further studied and taught abroad, and became ultimately Principal of Glasgow University.

John Or, appointed in 1559, was the first of a new type of schoolmaster. No longer were they clergymen for whom teaching was an additional duty, but laymen for whom teaching was a career. John Or was followed by Ninian Young (1572), William Murray (1595), Archibald Dunsmuire (1595), and William Wallace from Barnweil (1597).

Ayr burgh school after 1559 was not just a continuation of the old church school under new auspices. There was a deliberate and successful effort to extend its scope. In 1582 it was proposed that the council appoint 'ane skillit doctour' as an assistant to the master. The master of the grammar school would thereafter be able to concentrate on the teaching of Latin, while reading and writing were left to the 'doctor' as the assistant was called for the next 164 years. There was still, now as the third man, the master of the sang schule, which became known also as the Scots school or the English school. His duties were defined in 1583: 'to teiche the youths in the art of musik sufficientlie, and to learne them to sing, also to play upon the pynattis (spinet), and other instruments according to his knowledge, and to learne the bairns that sings to read and write Inglis, and shall sing in the kirk the four parts of musik.' Ayr was in fact devising here an elementary or primary department associated with the grammar school.

Throughout the 16th century the school continued at the Church of St John. But the church building was old and in need of repair. That part of it — perhaps an outbuilding — which formed the 'schule hous' had by 1599 been allowed to 'decay untheckit'. So in 1602 the town council decided to rent alternative accommodation: 'To John Osburn for 2 year mail of the Schoolhouse, £20 Scots.' Some local historians have presumed (wrongly) that the burgh school was 'a thatched house, with partitions, in the Sandgate.' In fact, as A.L. Taylor has proved, the school moved in 1602 from the Church of St John (where it had been for at least 369 years) to the present site (where it has remained for just about the same length of time).

THE SECOND SCHOOL: 1602 — 1800
THE BURGH SCHOOL

In 1602 the burgh school became established in a cottage, extending from east to west, situated near where the janitor's house now sits in the playground of the present Ayr Academy. The larger apartment was occupied by the master and doctor of the grammar school, and provided with desks and forms. The smaller 'chamber' to the west formed the sang school, with its own master.

In the new school a noteworthy advance was made. Girls as well as boys could be enrolled. It was decreed (in 1600) that 'the lasses that learne to read and write to be put to the master of the sang schule.' The grammar school was reserved for boys for 'it is not seemlie that sic lasses should be in the grammar school amang the lads.' This segregation was confirmed in 1604. All boys wishing schooling had to go to the grammar school unless they specially wished music. Girls were restricted to the sang schule, 'or any other school that pleases.' This tacitly allowed private schools to be set up for girls; but the private teaching of boys was still not allowed. Passing references suggest that while the burgh school catered for the children of the well-to-do, there were always private persons making a living by offering cheaper courses for some other girls and — despite the council's prohibition — for some boys too. The children of the poor, of course, went without any formal education.

A CENTURY OF PROBLEMS
The 17th century brought problems to Ayr. There were epidemics of plague in 1606 and 1647. A different kind of upset was caused by the religious disputes which convulsed the whole nation. Royal efforts to control the church led to resistance in the National Covenant of 1638, involvement in the English Civil War, and Cromwell's occupation of Scotland. Then between 1660 and 1689 the later Covenanters became involved in military uprisings and suffered persecution.

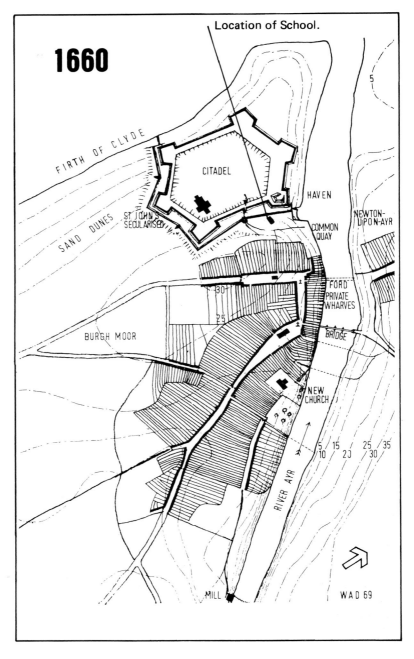

Location of School.

1660

FIRTH OF CLYDE

SAND DUNES

CITADEL

ST JOHN'S
SECULARISED

HAVEN

NEWTON-
UPON-AYR

COMMON
QUAY

FORD
PRIVATE
WHARVES

BURGH MOOR

BRIDGE

NEW
CHURCH

5 / 15   25 / 35
10 / 20 30

RIVER AYR

MILL

WAD 69

14

These civil and religious commotions did not leave the burgh school untouched. In 1652 Cromwell's army of occupation took over the Church of St John and made it part of the great fort or citadel that was constructed. Until 1655, when the new parish church off High Street was ready, church services were for three years held in the cramped conditions of the grammar school. After 1660 the work of the school was disrupted by the religious persecutions. In an earlier generation William Smyth, master of the grammar school, had signed the National Covenant. Now in 1675 William Wallace was forced to resign from that post because of his presbyterian principles and there were some difficulties over the appointment of David Skeoch as his successor. In 1676 James Anderson, doctor of the grammar school, was similarly forced to resign. Another master, William Rankin, was also put out in 1680 and re-admitted in 1684 after making an abject submission. Such incidents must have interrupted the work of the school. We can suspect that it was not always possible to keep the school fully staffed.

In 1642, for example, William Wallace had been dismissed for nonpolitical reasons, according to the presbytery records. 'The ministers . . . approved him in his Doctrine and facultie in teaching of the youth, and in the exercise of Discipline. But regretted his non attendance Diligentlie upon the school. The jarring and discord betwix him and the Doctor Robert Andro, quhilk was was likely to overthrowe the schoole. And also regretted the keiping back of some weil disposed shollers because of the dullness and ignorance of others.'

As far as can be judged from the incomplete local records, the following were masters of the grammar school: Alexander Dunsmuire (1605), John Bonar (1612), William Smyth (1638), William Wallace (1642), John Hamilton (1643), George Paterson (1649), Matthew Graham (1657), James Fleming (1664), William Wallace (1666— who, if the same person as the earlier one, was singularly unfortunate to be dismissed twice!), David Skeoch (1675), James Dickie (1676), William Rankin (1680). The only doctors of the grammar school known are: Robert Andrew (1642), John Hunter (1652), James Anderson (1673), James Dickie (1675), James Fergusson (1695). Known masters of the sang schule are: David Miller (1680), George Adamson (1695). There were several other teachers, though in which post is not known: Andrew Stewart (1652), Alexander Abercrombie (1664), John Wilson (1695).

This 'Prospect of the Town of Air from the East' of 1693 shows the second school as an isolated cottage left of the church.

16

Though the town council was obviously keen to staff its growing school, it had to find money to pay salaries in a period of rising prices. The original award of 12 merks or £8 in 1519 was increased to £20 when the council took over the school in 1559, raised to £40 in 1582, and by 1670 the figure was £200. These payments were in pounds Scots, only a fraction of sterling. The responsibilities of the several posts can be assessed in 1670: £200 to the master of the grammar school; around £130 to the doctor; and £60 to the master of the Scots (or sang) school. This money the council obtained from 'the common purse.'

Ayr was fortunate in having what was called Queen Mary's Mortification. During her reign, in 1567, various properties of the church were transferred to the council, and their rents were to be applied to various religious and charitable purposes. In times of financial stress, however, special measures had to be taken. In 1675 there was what appears to have been a special levy, and the inhabitants were 'stentit in four score punds yearly for the schoolmaster.' In 1690 the council had to borrow money to pay the masters.

More important to the teachers than their basic salaries paid by the council were the fees (or 'wages') paid by the pupils. The master of the grammar school took (in 1595) 20 shillings yearly from each 'Town's bairn' and 40 shillings from each landward pupil who came from outwith the burgh. The doctor charged lower fees of 8 shillings, and 13 shillings and fourpence. The master of the sang school (in 1597) charged 6 shillings and eightpence for singing, 13 shillings and four-pence for the spinet. Scholars were expected to pay quarterly in advance, bringing their 'quarter's scholage' to school. But the council had on occasion to collect fees, appointing visitors to call on defaulting parents. The fees of landward pupils could be claimed from the persons with whom they lodged in Ayr.

The incomes of the teachers could not have been particularly high. In time of famine or when money was short with parents or with the council, special provision had to be made. In 1591 the doctor could claim free meals from parents: 'his meit about of ilk bairn ane day successive.' Salaries were augmented in the 'great dearth' of 1596 and 1603. In 1613 the master of the sang school had his rent paid and was given a suit of clothes: 'chamber maill and a stand of clayths.'

In 1597 the master of the grammar school was given £10 to buy a gown. And each Candlemas, pupils brought gifts to their teachers.

The teachers had a supplementary source of income — fees paid to them for what were often vexatious duties they were expected to perform for the church. They were required to take charge of the children at church services and examine them afterwards, as part of their work. Fees were paid for other duties. The master of the grammar school was sometimes the Reader, assisting the minister with prayers and the lessons in the church services. He or the doctor was the Session Clerk, keeping a record of business, making lists of communicants, baptisms, marriages, and burials. The master of the sang school acted as Precentor, leading the congregation in singing the psalms. Because of this, the kirk session and the presbytery expected to be consulted by the council over the appointment of teachers, and after 1689 arranged ministerial visits to the school to examine pupils.

That education was highly regarded and the teachers held in respect is seen in 1613 when the master of the sang school was made honorary burgess and guild brother; and the same compliment was paid in 1677 to the master of the grammar school 'for the good service done in attending on the youths in the school.'

The 17th century saw another former pupil who made a name for himself. Andrew Michael Ramsay was born in 1686, the son of a baker who lived near the Fish Cross in High Street. From Ayr burgh school he went on to Edinburgh University, then went abroad, became a Roman Catholic, was a tutor to Prince Charles Edward Stuart, and a writer of various books which earned him fame as the 'Chevalier Ramsay'.

By the 18th century the burgh school was called upon to serve the needs of a growing town in an expanding economy. During the previous century the trade of the harbour had languished and by 1723 a visitor described Ayr as 'like a fine beauty in decay.' Now the harbour was renewed, public buildings renovated, old trades revived and new enterprises commenced. The population within the royal burgh doubled in the second half of the 18th century, reaching almost 4,000. The New Bridge, constructed between 1785 and 1788, provided better access from the even-more-rapidly growing areas north of the river. Newton-upon-Ayr, now with its own parish church and school, had nearly 2,000 inhabitants. Wallacetown (in St Quivox parish) had 1,000 inhabitants, with a parish school since 1699. This community of seven thousand persons had its prosperous merchants and trades-folk who required an appropriate education for their sons and daughters; and from the county came children of landowners whose agricultural improvements were proving so successful. Ayr town council throughout the century made valiant efforts to extend its educational provision. The burgh school had to be staffed with sufficient and competent teachers. The two-roomed schoolhouse was extended in 1721 and again in 1747. And the curriculum had to be widened.

Between 1708 and 1746 the master of the grammar school was James Fergusson, a local man who had already been teaching for thirteen years as the doctor, and was promoted after William Rankin's death — to serve the school altogether for some fifty years. Sometime during Fergusson's career, accommodation was doubled by constructing a new cottage parallel to the old school building on its north or harbour side. This was probably in 1721 when the doctor, Thomas Alstoun, was instructed to accomplish himself in 'the mathematical sciences' and the new building became known as the Mathematical School.

JOHN MAIR
In 1727 to this new department came John Mair, one of Ayr's greatest masters. In that year the council advertised for a 'doctor of superior qualifications.' The candidates had to undergo a searching three-day examination. John Hall was appointed by the provost's casting vote, but when he withdrew the appointment went to John Mair. Mair was a St Andrews graduate who was Hall's equal in four subjects, superior in navigation, but less skilled in handwriting (which he promised to improve). John Mair turned out to be a most competent and enthusiastic innovator, who was able to offer a wide range of subjects, almost certainly as wide as in any burgh school in Scotland. Some had been previously provided. To the traditional reading and writing, arithmetic had been added here in 1673. Book-keeping had been introduced in 1716. Mathematics, begun in 1721, was developed for 'as the world now knows, the mathematical part

of learning is a principal part of a gentleman's education.' Mair could cope with all these subjects, and added navigation and geography from 1729. The council supplied 'maps and globes, the knowledge of which . . . is highly necessary for forming the man of business.' Around the same time is the first mention of the teaching of Greek, in 1727.

The master of the grammar school earning £200 Scots and the doctor at £100, both plus fees, were much better off than the English master in the sang school who had only £40. Some of the English masters of a previous generation had pioneered instruction in arithmetic (1673), painting and drawing (1673), playing on the spinet (1627), and latterly book-keeping and 'fine wryting' (1716). But by 1730 the English master was over-burdened by church duties — session clerk, precentor, keeper of clocks and collector of the poors rate. In 1739 he was found wanting and dismissed as 'not known in the new method of teaching English.' By this time there were only twenty pupils left in the sang school. Private schools were being tacitly recognised, provided they limited themselves to teaching reading and writing.

1746 is a key-date in the school's history. In that year the council generously sent old John Fergusson into retirement on full pay — 'aged, valetudinary, tender, and much afflicted with the gout or gravel . . . continued his yearly salary during the short time he may now live.' John Mair was the obvious choice as his successor, and he took the opportunity to propose that the burgh school be converted into what he called 'a sort of academy.' The council implemented his plan and awarded John Mair the new title of Rector, to be intimated publicly 'by beat of drum.' Mair continued his own specialist subjects — arithmetic, book-keeping, geography, navigation, surveying, Euclid's elements, algebra and other mathematical sciences, plus some natural philosophy, as well as taking the top class in Latin. A second master (the old title of doctor was now dropped) would be responsible for the five junior classes in Latin and for Greek. Archibald Wallace from Cumnock was appointed. A new English master, James Baillie from Irvine, would teach reading, using the 'new method.' In 1751 a fourth post was created. William Robinson would be Writing master responsible for elementary instruction in reading, writing, vulgar arithmetic, and music. He continued here and as precentor in the parish church — where he introduced 'the new music' — till he resigned in 1782.

There was a proposal to build a new English schoolhouse in High Street. In fact in 1747 the two existing buildings of the school were linked by building an English schoolroom between the old two-roomed grammar school and the newer mathematical room. Ayr burgh school now possessed a rector and three other masters in the extended four-room schoolhouse. John Mair — the last doctor and first rector in Ayr, the first science teacher in Scotland, headmaster of what was in fact if not yet in name the first academy in Scotland — could now, in the words of A.L. Taylor, 'perambulate his little kingdom at all seasons without exposing himself to the rigours of the Scottish climate.'

By the second half of the 18th century it is possible for the first time to get some insight into what school life was like — thanks to the painstaking study of this period by A.L. Taylor. Pupils selected a number of classes and attended only at the appropriate times. School hours for English were 9—12 and 2—4 (1—3 in winter) for six days in the week. Latin was taught from 7—9, 10—12 (9—12 in winter) and 2—4. The hours for mathematics were 9—12 and 2—4 or 5. Because one of the two rooms in the grammar school was so small it was necessary to squeeze in writing and drawing in the larger room from 12-3. The teaching of French (from 1761) could be arranged only outwith school hours. Astronomy (1761) was available as an evening class. In addition to this six-day timetable, the English master was expected to take a class on the principles of the Christian religion on Sundays after the afternoon church service. We can guess at a total school roll of around 150 pupils. There were about 60 in the grammar school and rather more in the English school.

A new scale of charges was determined. There were quarterly fees for reading, 3/-; writing, 2/6; Latin, 5/-. In other subjects the fees were for a complete course. Arithmetic to the single rule of three cost 5/-; the whole of vulgar arithmetic, 10/6; decimal arithmetic, 10/6; bookkeeping with the first set of books, 10/6; a full course, one guinea; navigation, one guinea; mathematics including Euclid, trigonometry, practical geometry and algebra, two guineas; natural philosophy, two guineas. Experimental work in natural philosophy required apparatus. In 1773 the town council paid for an 'electorizing machine' and 'crystal receiver to the air pump and tubes for mathematical demonstrations.' In 1776 they provided two wheels for 'the electorizing machine, two horizontal and vertical axes, a pedestal for vertical axis screws and for repairing the same, furnishing a new intermitting foundation, tan tubes cup to fit the side of the large conductor, and for soldering the spiers of the air pump.'

The scholars when not in class played handball on the town green, until damage to slates and windows of the school in 1775 resulted in prohibition, with a massive £3 fine for any infringement. The summer holidays were in June, if the town council adopted Mair's recommendation in 1747. May he adjudged too cold, and then boys would 'often run great hazards' by bird-nesting. In June some scholars already went to Arran 'and other distant places' to drink goats milk. Pupils from Carrick and Galloway did not usually arrive till after the June fair. On the last day before the holidays was Examination Day, fixed in 1766 on the second Thursday in June. Visiting councillors and ministers examined the proficiency of all pupils, and in 1787 the provost introduced prizes for the best scholars. There was at the same time an inspection of the mathematical and scientific apparatus and of the library. This was the Ayr Library which was founded in 1762, and though for private subscribers was housed in the burgh school with the English master as librarian.

In 1761 John Mair went off to introduce the educational ideas he had been operating in Ayr, as Rector of Perth Academy, the first school in Scotland to be thus styled. Mair's successor at Ayr retained the title of rector and the powers of headmaster — 'He shall have the Inspection of the School.' But thereafter the council reverted to the traditional arrangement of several masters operating virtually independent departments with no one in overall charge.

AT THE TIME OF BURNS
Alexander Paterson who succeeded as rector in 1761 had come from Tranent as Latin master in 1751. Originating in the north east, he became acquainted with William Burnes, another incomer from that airt. Even after Paterson's death in 1768 his widow lent William Burnes books for the use of his son Robert. Arthur Oughterson succeeded as Latin master in 1761 and as Master of the grammar school from 1768 till 1771. He was followed briefly by John Inglis.

22

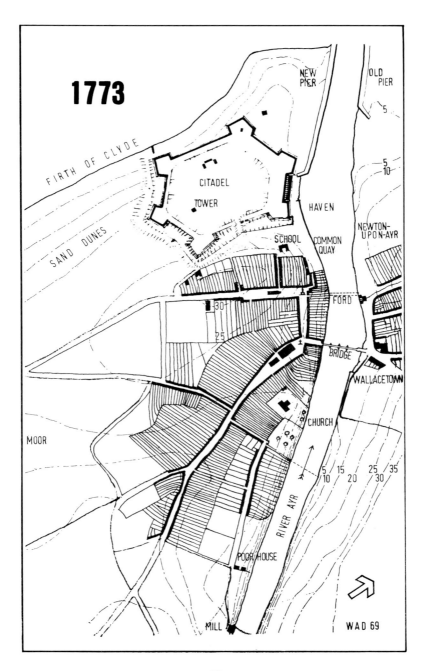

1773

FIRTH OF CLYDE

NEW PIER

OLD PIER

5

5
10

SAND DUNES

CITADEL
TOWER

HAVEN

NEWTON-
UPON-AYR

SCHOOL

COMMON
QUAY

30

25

FORD

BRIDGE

WALLACETOWN

MOOR

CHURCH

5   15   25   35
  10   20   30

RIVER AYR

POOR HOUSE

MILL

WAD 69

23

In 1772 came another long memorable term of office. David Tennant, a virtually self-taught lad from Alloway, was appointed English master in 1755 at the age of 21. In 1769 he introduced 'English grammer, which was a branch almost entirely new.' In 1772 after 'strict and sufficient trial' he was appointed master of the grammar school. Previously in 1765 Tennant had recommended to William Burnes an 18-year-old pupil, John Murdoch, as a suitable person to conduct a little school at Alloway, where Robert Burns was his pupil till Murdoch went off to Dumfries in 1768. Now in 1772 John Murdoch returned to Ayr to fill the vacancy of English master, renewed his acquaintance with the Burnes family, and for three weeks in the autumn of 1773 enrolled 14-year-old Robert Burns as a pupil to 'perfect his grammar' and introduced him to French. William Robinson, the Writing master, advised Burns to begin the study of Latin. But Murdoch's stay in Ayr was brief. He was unwise enough to criticise the authorities for alleged mismanagement of the school while he was 'overtaken in liquor.' He was dismissed in 1776 and went off to London.

In 1773, to extend facilities, the town council appointed John Hunter from New Galloway as a second English master. They installed him in a new separate schoolhouse in High Street behind the Wallace Tower. This was a stone-built erection, 50 feet long, 20 feet broad, 12 feet high, with five windows in the rear, and four and a door in front. This did not prove a success. When Hunter took over Murdoch's job in 1775, his successor William Neill from Monkton found the Wallace Tower school inconvenient and took his pupils in his own house further down the High Street by the Fish Cross.

Things certainly were not going smoothly at this time. David Tennant as master of the grammar school had no authority outwith his own department. The various masters were competing against one another to secure pupils. The advanced mathematical and scientific studies initiated by Mair were languishing. George Douglas came from Edinburgh in 1768 as Mathematics master. But though he produced a book on the **Elements of Euclid** in 1776, he was found wanting as a teacher. He was suspended in 1784 for 'want of authority' and dismissed in 1791. Alexander Carson, the Writing master appointed in 1782, had to be asked to retire in 1790; and his successor William MacKenzie from

Kirkcudbright lasted only two years. In 1792 the two English masters (Hunter and Neill) and the Mathematical master (James Morton who had replaced Douglas) had to be asked to desist from teaching writing — an indication that they were spending too much time on elementary work to the neglect of their specialist subjects.

With the burgh school in such an unhappy state, private schools were flourishing. The town council abandoned its traditional attempts to suppress them. Indeed the council began to patronise private schools for girls. In 1764 they bestowed a grant on a lady who taught 'sewing, embroidery and other accomplishments proper for that sex.' In 1782 an annual grant was offered to two sisters who kept a boarding school for the daughters of gentlemen.

Throughout the 18th century one outstanding source of friction continued to add to difficulties — relations between the town council (which was responsible for finance and administration of the burgh school) and the church (which claimed certain control over staff and curriculum). The better-paid masters sought wherever possible to shed their church duties, leaving their more poorly-paid colleagues over-burdened. One particular vexation arose when Rev. John Hunter published a Latin grammar in 1711 and kept trying to have it introduced into the grammar school. In 1732 Fergusson and Mair succeeded in having its continued use prohibited. Mair went on to publish his own **Introduction to Latin Syntax** in 1755. (He also produced a work on book-keeping which has become internationally recognised as a pioneer contribution to accountancy methods). It seems probable that certain members of the presbytery would be less than keen on the modern studies then being introduced, like Mair's experimental science and (perhaps) Murdoch's French.

Sir

*I am no stranger to your friendly offices in my
Publication; and had that been the only debt I owed you, I
would long since have acknowledged it; as the next Merchant's
phrase, dressed up a little, would have served my purpose.*

*But there is a certain cordial, friendly welcome in my
reception, when I meet with you; an apparent heart warm
honest joy at having it in your power to befriend a man
whose abilities you were pleased to honor with some degree
of applause— befriending him in the very way too most
flattering to his feelings, by handing him up to that dear
lov'd Notice of the World — this, Sir, I assure you
with brimful eyes this moment, I have often wished to
thank you for, but was as often at a loss for expression
suitable to the state of my heart. God knows I know
very little of great folks; and I hope He can be
my witness, that for meer Greatness, I as little care.
Worth, in whatever circumstances, I prize; but Worth
conjoined with Greatness, has a certain irresistable power
of attracting esteem. ——*

*I have taken the liberty to inscribe the inclosed Poem
to you. — I am the more at ease about this, as it is*

LETTER TO JOHN BALLANTINE, ESQ., AYR.
FROM ROBERT BURNS.
(With "The Brigs of Ayr")

Sir,

I am no stranger to your friendly offices in my Publication; and had that been the only debt I owed you, I would long since have acknowledged it; as the next Merchant's phrase, dressed up a little, would have served my purpose.

But there is a certain cordial, friendly welcome in my reception, when I meet with you; an apparent heart warm, honest joy at having it in you power to befriend a man whose abilities you were pleased to honor with some degree of applause—befriending him in the very way too most flattering to his feelings, by handing him up to that dear lov'd NOTICE OF THE WORLD—This, Sir, I assure you with brimful eyes this moment, I have often wished to thank you for, but was as often at a loss for expression suitable to the state of my heart. God knows I know very little of GREAT FOLKS: and I hope He can be my witness, that for meer Greatness I as little care.

Worth, in whatever circumstances, I prize; but Worth conjoined with Greatness has a certain irresistable power of attracting esteem.

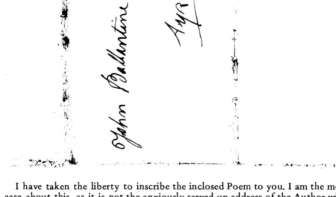

I have taken the liberty to inscribe the inclosed Poem to you. I am the more at ease about this, as it is not the anxiously served up address of the Author wishing to conciliate a liberal Patron; but the honest Sincerity of heart-felt Gratitude. Of its merits I shall say nothing; as I can truly say that whatever applauses it could recieve would not give me so much pleasure as having it in my power, in the way I like best, to assure you how sincerely I am,

    Sir,

your much indebted humble serv^t.
ROBERT BURNS.

Mossgiel, 27th Sept. 1786.

PLANNING AN ACADEMY

However, the council and others in the town were converted to John Mair's prophetic vision in 1746 of 'a sort of academy where almost every sort of the more useful kinds of Literature will be taught and the want of College education will in great measure be supplied to boys whose parents cannot well afford to maintain them at Universities. Gentlemen in the County will be encouraged to send their children to Ayr, considering that the school will by this means have no rival.'

In 1791 a bequest from John Fergusson of Doonholm provided the opportunity. This was a grandson of that James Fergusson who had served as master of the grammar school till 1746, and a nephew of the 'worthy gentleman' who had employed Robert Burns' father. To augment the generous Fergusson bequest of £1000 and the £100 annually donated by Ayr town council, subscriptions were invited to finance the construction of a new school and the creation of an Academy.

Proposals issued in 1794 pointed out the advantage of 'a good Education.' Study at Universities could be 'tedious and expensive . . . (producing) speculative and idolent habits . . . ill-suited to the circumstances of the great bulk of the people in a commercial country.' But a local academy would offer 'the most necessary and useful parts of learning . . . under the observation of their parents and friends . . . furnished with teachers of approved ability.'

Fifty six gentlemen, tempted by the promise of hereditary directorships, contributed over £50 each, and altogether there were over two hundred subscribers. A third of them came from Ayr itself; another third were county gentry; the others were old boys living elsewhere, many in India and Jamaica.

In 1798 a royal charter for the establishment of 'the Academy of Air' was granted on behalf of King George III to John Ballantine, Provost of Ayr, who was elected first chairman of the Board of Directors. It was Ballantine's drive and enthusiasm which brought to reality the academy as first conceived by John Mair.

AYR. July 24th 1812.

On Monday the 20th inst. were interred in the family burial ground here with every mark of PUBLIC RESPECT, the remains of John Ballantine Esqr: of Castlehill: a Gentleman who was never more endeared to his private friends by his Unassuming Manners, and Amiable Dispositions, than to the Community of which he was long the Head, by his Exertions for the Improvement of his NATIVE PLACE.

Of these, are ELEGANT BRIDGE, and that highly beneficial institution, the ACADEMY, (will remain lasting Monuments.)

The former was erected during his Administration; and of the latter, he may be said to have been THE FOUNDER.

29

No. 1

WE, the Subscribers, promise and oblige ourselves, to pay the Sums annexed to our respective Subscriptions, to the Treasurer who shall be appointed by the Committee named for establishing Schools at AIR for the Instruction of Youth; and that, as soon as it shall be certified by the said Committee, by Advertisements in the Edinburgh Newspapers, that a Sum sufficient for such an Establishment is actually Subscribed.

First page of Subscription List, 1794.

30

Already on 1st August 1796 the first session of Ayr Academy began in the old burgh school premises, while plans were made for a new building to be erected beside it on the School Green. John Robertson of Glasgow was engaged as architect and James Miller was contractor. The cost would be £3,000 and it was to be ready by the last day of 1799.

To take charge of the Academy someone of outstanding qualifications was sought, and offered a salary of £80 per year, plus £20 for taking in boarders, plus his share of fees. William Meikleham was in 1796 appointed first Rector of Ayr Academy. A Kilmarnock man, he had been lecturing at Glasgow University, which awarded him a doctorate, and in 1799 appointed him as professor of astronomy. So after only three years a second rector arrived, another highly-qualified scientist, Thomas Jackson, in time to see the move into the new academy building.

In staffing the academy the departmental system of the burgh school was retained, but the masters were nearly all new. David Tennant, the poorly-qualified but much-experienced master of the grammar school, was retained as Classical master till his eventual retiral in 1811 after 56 years' service. As Writing and Drawing master, Robert Taylor was appointed, previously tutor to the Earl of Dumfries. As a native of England he was thought fit to begin additional classes in elocution in 1805. David Ballingal was appointed Mathematical master; applied for the rectorship in 1799; and was successful in 1809 when Jackson resigned to become professor of natural philosophy at St Andrews. For the remaining posts, English and French, it was essential, the directors decided, that the masters be natives of those countries. Andrew Paterson was appointed English master in 1799. As master of Modern Languages, a Monsieur Dohin was appointed in 1797, followed between 1802 and 1810 by the Abbe Nicolas — of whom more later. What of the two men who had been English masters in the burgh school? They were not thought 'capable of teaching English pronounciation and Grammar.' So John Hunter and William Neill, though allowed to continue teaching in premises in the High Street, under patronage of the town council, were not accepted as members of the academy staff.

Evening Courant

JUNE 9. 1796. PRICE FOURPENCE.

This Day is Published,
BY MUNDELL & SON,
Parliament Stairs ;

And to be had also at the shops of Mess. James Dickson, John Guthrie, John Fairbairn, Peter Hill, John Ogle, Manners and Miller, and Archibald Constable, in one volume 8vo. price 5s. in boards,

THE LIFE of SAMUEL JOHNSON, L.L.D.

With Critical Observations on his Works.

BY ROBERT ANDERSON, M.D.

This Life is prefixed to Johnson's Works, in Anderson's Edition of the Poets.

" We may venture to say, on the whole, that this work, which we have examined with much pleasure, is written with strength, elegance, good taste, and found judgment" Monthly Review for May 1795.—See also the British Critic, Analytical and Critical Reviews for January.

Also, in 13 volumes Royal Octavo,
price 8l. in boards,

THE WORKS OF THE BRITISH POETS,
With Prefaces Biographical and Critical.

BY ROBERT ANDERSON.

This is by far the most comprehensive edition of the British Poets ever published, and contains the whole Poetical Writings of 113 different Authors, beginning with Chaucer, and ending with Blacklocke.—Lists of whom may be had of the Publishers.

" We consider the present work as a valuable acquisition to English Literature. As a collection of British Poetry and Biography, it confers honour upon the Editor, for genius, taste, and information, tending to promote and perpetuate the most imperishable monument of Britain's glory."— British Critic for February 1796.

N.B. The Poetical translations for which distinct titles were printed, may be had separately in two volumes royal octavo, price 1l. 2s. in boards.

To be had as above, in 3 vols. 12mo. price 6s. bound,
THE POEMS OF OSSIAN THE SON OF FINGAL,
Translated by Jam s Macpherson, Esq.

ALSO,

Rollin's Ancient History, 10 vols. 12mo. (plates) price 35s. bound.

A Summary View of Heraldry, &c. by Thomas Brydson, F.A.S. Edinburgh, royal 8vo, price 10s. 6d. in boards.

Potter's Antiquities of Greece, 2 vols. 8vo, price 14s. in boards.

Locke on the Human Understanding, 3 vols. 12mo, price 9s. bound.

Rousseau's Eloisa (Dr Kenrick's Translation), 3 vols. 12mo, price 10s. 6d. bound

Clarke and Pyle's Paraphrase, forming a complete Commentary on the New Testament, 2 vols. 8vo, price 30s. in boards.

Young's whole Works, with his Life, by Robert Anderson, M.D. 3 vols. 12mo, price 10s. 6d. bound.

Mandeville's Fable of the Bees, 2 vols. price 8s. bound.

Beaumont's Misses Magazine, 2 vols. 12mo, price 4s. bound.

Mrs Rowe's whole Works, with her Life prefixed, 4 vols. small 8vo, price 14s. bound.

Blair's (Author of the Grave) Poems, with his Life, by Robert Anderson, M.D. price 1s. sewed.

⁕ A good assortment of LONDON ARTICLES, with which the Trade may be supplied.—NEW BOOKS of note brought down regularly as published.

EQUIVALENT OFFICE,
JUNE 1. 1796.

THE COURT OF DIRECTORS of the EQUIVALENT COMPANY give notice, That a General Court of the said Company will be held at their house, No. 2, Copthall Buildings, near Throgmorton Street, London, on Wednesday the 6th of July next, at one o'clock at noon precisely, on special affairs.

And they also give notice, That the Transfer Books of the said Company will be shut on Wednesday the 8th inst. and continue to till Wednesday the 13th of July next.

PAUL BAXTER & COMPANY
RESPECTFULLY OFFER

Their Grateful Acknowledgments to the Public and their Friends, for the numerous Favours they have conferred on them and their Family, during a period of near 30 years, in connection with the respectable House of Mess. Hesland, Elder, and Co.—

HAVING now commenced BUSINESS for themselves, in the
CONFECTIONERY, & { PATENT MEDICINE LINE,
GROCERY, }

They humbly solicit a continuance of the same liberal patronage and support; which they shall study to merit, by keeping always Goods of the best Quality, and on Low Terms.
College Street, June 1. 1796.

TO THE FREEHOLDERS OF THE COUNTY OF AYR.

COLONEL FULLARTON having been detained longer in London than he expected, has not had an opportunity of late, of waiting personally on his Friends, the Freeholders of Ayrshire ; and as the Sheriff has fixed Friday the 17th of June curt. for electing a Representative in Parliament for that County, he takes this public manner of intimating the time of election, and requests the attendance of all the Freeholders who are to honour him with their support, at Ayr, early in the morning of the 17th of June, at the house of Mrs Simpson vintner, Ayr.

TO THE FREEHOLDERS OF THE COUNTY OF PERTH.

GENTLEMEN,

COLONEL GRAHAM having, before he left Scotland, desired us, in case he should be necessarily absent on the day of Election, to pay attention to his Friends on that occasion, we beg leave to request the honour of your attendance at Perth, on Saturday the 18th curt. the day appointed by the Sheriff for the choice of a Member for the County, when we trust that Colonel Graham's friends, if not particularly engaged, will honour him with their personal support.

DAVID SMYTH—and for
JAMES TOWNSEND OSWALD.
Edinburgh, June 7. 1796.

Mr HERON of HERON.

WITH his most respectful Compliments to the FREEHOLDERS of the STEWARDRY of KIRKCUDBRIGHT, earnestly requests the honour of their attendance at Kirkcudbright upon Tuesday the 21st curt. the day fixed by the Steward Depute for the election of a Member to serve in Parliament for their county, at the head of the Election.
Edinburgh, June 3. 1796.

AYR ACADEMY,
UNDER THE DIRECTION OF
WILLIAM MEIKLEHAM, A. M. RECTOR,
Who, for the greater part of two years past, has taught, with success and reputation, the Natural Philosophy in the University of Glasgow.

THIS Institution will commence on MONDAY the first day of AUGUST next, in which will be taught the different Branches of Education formerly stated in the Professors, viz.

ARITHMETIC,
BOOK KEEPING,
GEOGRAPHY, with the Use of the Globes,
EUCLID'S ELEMENTS,
TRIGONOMETRY, Plane and Spherical,
MENSURATION, and other Practical Branches of the Mathematics, } by Mr Meikleham, and his Assistants.
GUNNERY and FORTIFICATION,
NATURAL PHILOSOPHY, in which will be included ASTRONOMY, &c. for the illustration of which, by Experiments, a complete Apparatus of Instruments is provided,
LATIN and GREEK, } Mr David Tennant.
WRITING and DRAWING, } Mr Robert Taylor.
ENGLISH, FRENCH, ITALIAN, &c. } by proper Masters, native of England and France.

The Managers of this Institution, being in possession of very considerable Funds, which they have good reason to believe will soon be greatly augmented, are of opinion, that the course of Education which is to be carried on in this Seminary may now be commenced with such a plan as will be found to comprehend such branches as to render it fully sufficient for those who are inclined for the learned professions ; and, that it will remove the inconveniences necessarily connected with the sending of youth for the above branches of Education to distant Universities.

From the acknowledged abilities and fidelity of the Teachers who are engaged in this Institution, with the determined resolution of the Managers to do every thing in their power to support it ; the healthful situation of the town of Ayr ; its central position in a large and populous country ; and the excellence and cheapness of its markets, there is good reason to hope that every purpose intended by this Establishment will be fully answered.

In November next, Mr Meikleham will be ready to receive BOARDERS on moderate terms, on the superintendance of whole Education he will bestow the utmost attention. Mr Meikleham will also teach a CLASS for GREEK and ROMAN ANTIQUITIES, and for pointing out the Beauties and Elegancies of these Languages.
Published by direction of the Committee,
May 9. 1796. JOHN BALLANTINE, Convener.

THE FOLLOWING

THE THIRD SCHOOL: 1800 — 1880
THE OLD ACADEMY

What became known as the 'Old Academy' was opened in stages from July 1799 to January 1800. As compared with 269 crammed into the old school at the beginning of that session, 374 scholars were enrolled in the academy a year later. Numbers grew rapidly to 480 in 1804 and reached a maximum of 594 in 1829.

The Academy was in Fort Street, set well back in a broad playground behind a wall with iron railings and a central gate, just south of the old burgh school which could now be demolished after its two centuries' life. The new two-storey building was judged 'plain and not very ornamental . . . chaste, and in good taste.' It had accommodation for the rector's classes and those of the other five masters. There was a 'lofty and spacious' hall, with a gallery, and a little tower for use as an observatory. An orrery, telescope, and in all £300 worth of astronomical equipment had been ordered by Dr Meikleham. A janitor was appointed. A janitor's lodge at the gate was planned, but was not built till 1842. The janitor's family was expected to assist with the cleaning of the school. He was forbidden to sell liquor.

The Old Ayr Academy.

THE Secretary laid before the Meeting the following Letter, or Report from the Rector:—

"AIR ACADEMY, 2d May, 1808.

SIR,

"AGREEABLE to your desire I now lay before you, for the information of the Directors of the Air Academy, the number of the Scholars attending at present each of the Schools in that Seminary.

	Boys.	Girls.	Total.
English	95	45	140
Writing	147	45	192
Arithmetic	115	20	135
French	40	6	46
Grammar School	107	—	107
Geography	15	—	15
Mathematics	14	—	14
Composition	6	—	6
Natural Philosophy	5	—	5
Chemistry	9	—	9
Drawing	—	—	11

"I cannot refrain from congratulating my constituents, the very respectable Founders and Patrons of this Institution, on its gradually progressive and present flourishing condition. The number of Scholars enrolled this year considerably exceeds the highest number of any former year, at the same period of the Session. In several of the more generally useful departments, indeed, the number has now become so great, as to render assistants absolutely necessary. When the Directors consider how fluctuating every institution of this kind must be, and the consequent risk as well as heavy expence * incurred by the Masters in procuring Assistants, they will no doubt see the necessity of endeavouring to supply some of the Masters with a fund to defray, at least a part of that expence. Any arrangement of an opposite nature or tendency might essentially injure the prosperity of the Institution, and would not so well accord with the generosity of the Directors, as a requital for the zeal and persevering exertions to which that prosperity seems to be in a great measure due. That something must be done in consequence of the great increase of the number of Students is obvious : what that shall be it is for the wisdom of the Directors to decide. The difficulty of making an unobjectionable arrangement my official situation gives me the fullest opportunity of perceiving, and requires me to state."

I have the honour to be, with much respect,

SIR,

Your most obedient servant,

THOs. JACKSON.

George Dunlop, Esq. Provost of Air.

* The English Master pays at present for an Assistant £45 ; The Master of the Grammar School, nearly as much ; and the Writing Master, nearly £30 for two Assistants.

The rector had still only a 'general supervision of the schools.' He and two directors were expected to visit the various classes every three months. Apart from this, he would have 'little connection with the Masters.' They would teach their own subjects (apart from those classes allocated to the rector by the directors) and be in virtually independent control of their own departments, of which they were indeed sometimes described as 'headmasters'. Like the rector they could arrange to hire ushers to assist them in their teaching, and make their own approaches to the Board of Directors. Each arranged five or six hour-long classes meeting daily between the hours of 8 a.m. and 4 p.m. Scholars might enrol for one class only, or more usually for one in several departments.

On the first Monday in August and each Saturday morning throughout the session the entire school met in a general assembly following the ringing of the town bell. There the progress of individual pupils was noted and conduct assessed. Pupils might be disciplined for the following misdemeanours: absence from class, lateness, lesson unprepared, making noise near school, throwing stones, defacing walls, malicious gossip, falsehood, habitual swearing, absence from divine service, carrying a stick or staff, use of fire-arms, going into boats, disrespectful behaviour. Punishments included reprimands, tasks at home, seats of disgrace, temporary confinements, fines, corporal punishment, expulsion.

At the very end of the session was Examination Day. The provost's prizes instituted in 1787 were supplement from 1797 onwards by the directors who offered 'small honorary premiums' to 'the most deserving scholars.' In 1807 silver medals were awarded by John Johnstone because of the 'advantages which my numerous family has derived from this institution.' There survive numerous examples of such awards. The earliest is a copy of Goldsmith's **History of England** inscribed: 'May 1799. Given by the directors to James Dunlop for having acquired a superior knowledge in Arithmetic & Book-keeping to the rest of his class Fellows.' There is an 1808 silver medal for the Elocution class.

PUNISHMENTS
There also survive some recollections of the early days of the academy. One boy who enrolled in September 1799 at the age of six, when the new building was not yet complete, remembered especially the harshness of the punishments. Mr Paterson, the English master, was unusually lax in that he only made disobedient boys put on a large wig. The 'English teacher of the old school' — presumably John Hunter — was quite severe. He punished boys after they were tied down on a special bench he called his 'mare' with the aid of two pupils nominated as 'grooms', one called Mossman and the other a black African called William Barton. The Latin master after 1811, Ebenezer Thomson, was also regarded as a harsh

35

disciplinarian. After two particularly severe floggings were reported to the directors in 1814 he was advised to make use only of 'leathern thongs commonly denominated Tawse.' But the most noted exponent of corporal punishment in the history of the academy was undoubtedly the long-serving Writing and Drawing master, Robert Taylor.

One well-documented occasion was in 1807 when, because of new holiday arrangements, the school met during the Ayr Races. 'A number of boys, and I among them, set this new rule at defiance, and went to the Races. No doubt this was very wrong, but we were all prepared to receive punishment in extinction of the offence. I was reported as one of the culprits, and unfortunately for me, the time of my writing lesson was during the young ladies' hour. On my walking into the school, I was at once called up, but what was my surprise to be told, that if I would give up the names of the other boys who had been at the Races, I should receive a free pardon! To any one accustomed to the Free Masonry that reigns among boys, it is unnecessary to explain that such a proposal was quite inadmissable. Being rejected by me the master proceeded to his desk, and brought out his formidable whip, which in order to make it more pungent was twisted round with the hard cord used for tying up the bundles of quill pens. He caught me by the arm, and swung me round him, thrashing me severely from shoulder to heel. I was determined not to give in or shed a tear in presence of the girls, and I do believe he would soon have ceased, but a Miss Robertson called out by way of encouragement to me, "Stand firm," which so provoked him that he renewed his efforts till I had received over fifty lashes. I then, in despair, threw myself round him and sank my teeth in the calf of his leg, from which the blood ran down his stocking! No doubt this was very wrong on my part, and very bad behaviour, yet even now I cannot help thinking it was excusable.' Taylor's punishment of the boy was not criticised by the directors, but he was persuaded to withdraw a demand that the boy should be expelled for assaulting a master. Taylor's strong-arm methods are confirmed by another former pupil who admitted that he could never show his son where he had been thrashed. That girls were not immune is revealed in a letter of 13th December, 1824 from a parent complaining that his daughter had been struck in the face with a book 'which bled one eye, and blackened both.' On returning to school she was 'taken by the hair, by the throat, and pulled about in a way unknown in modern schools, and sent home in a state of high fever.' To assist in his everyday discipline, Taylor had a 'censor' for each form in his classroom.

ROBERT TAYLOR AND OTHER MASTERS

'Auld Robin' was accounted a good teacher and was 'much respected.' Samples of his own work and copy books of some of his best pupils have been preserved. His skill as a draughtsman he once tested. He made a copy of a pound note and presented it in a bank. The clerk changed it and was astonished when Taylor returned the money.

Robert Taylor

For sixty four years Robert Taylor taught writing (with his brother 'Wee John' sharpening the quill pens), drawing, and elocution. By the time he retired in 1858 half the directors were old pupils of his. Though there was no requirement to provide a pension, the directors generously awarded him an annuity of £50 a year. A public subscription produced the considerable sum of £465 for his 'long and zealous services.'

The long tenure of Robert Taylor as Writing and Drawing master (1794–1855) was followed by another, that of Laurence Anderson (1855–1902). He was appointed as Writing master, for in drawing there had been an 'absence of late years of all provision.' Yet within a few years he was in charge of what was now called the Art Department and himself held in 'high esteem.'

Noteworthy developments occurred also in the other departments of the academy.

The Classical master, David Tennant, after 56 years of teaching, now with an 'impediment in hearing . . . feeling perceptibly the effects of age' retired in 1833. He was

Collection

OF

more than three hundred

ORIGINAL

Charades, Enigmas,

Anagrams, Palindromes, Conundrums,

REBUSES,

&

Anomalous Riddles,

composed by

Robert Taylor

of the

Academy

AYR.

Specimen of Robert Taylor's written work.

Yesterday cannot be recalled.

Yesterday cannot be recalled.

Yesterday cannot be recalled.

Yesterday cannot be recalled.

Yesterday cannot be recalled.

A.G. Donaldson

Pupil's writing exercise, 1819.

succeeded by Ebenezer Thomson, already noted as a strict disciplinarian. He was also a man of considerable erudition. He published a scholarly edition of **The Kingis Quhair** in 1816. He was an enthusiast for Old English and produced an **Anglo Saxon Grammar** in 1832. He held adult evening classes on the language, and was even able to persuade some boys to attend a class on the subject at 7 a.m. After Thomson's retiral in 1838 and in view of the 'diminution of classical education throughout Scotland' the rector took over the Latin and Greek classes and the separate Classics department was temporarily abolished.

When the academy's first English master, James Paterson, resigned he was followed by James Ridley (1819—34). A popular teacher of English and elocution who came from St Andrews, Ridley replaced Paterson's Lancastrian methods with the teaching system of Dr Andrew Bell, 'the author of the greatest improvement perhaps ever made in general education.' After fourteen successful years he died. He was followed by Arthur Lang (1838—66) whose lack of discipline caused the directors some concern. If a pupil required to be punished, Lang delegated the unpleasant duty to an assistant. After his retiral the next English master was George Hall (1866—71) who would become headmaster of Ayr's new elementary Grammar School; then William Wyllie (1871—73) and William Cormack (1873—95).

Of the Mathematics masters, David Ballingal became rector in 1809. James Gray, perhaps appropriately known as 'Fisty', taught for 46 years till his retiral in 1846. The next two masters after short stays left for better posts. Archibald Montgomerie from Manchester left in 1858 to become rector at Greenock. John Shand from Gosport (1858 —68) became eventually professor of mathematics and natural philosophy at Otago University and survived till 1915. He was followed by James Thomson from Irvine.

The policy of employing a foreigner to teach modern languages was followed for a long time. French with some Italian was offered by Mr Dohin followed by the Abbe Nicolas (1802—10), a man of initiative and personality whose career is worth noting here. Francois Leonar Olivier Nicolas was a native of Lisieux in Normandy. In 1788 he became a priest and one of the cathedral clergy in his native place. When the French Revolution made things difficult, the Abbe

39

Nicolas like many other churchmen left in 1792 for England. He moved to Paisley, supporting himself by teaching and providing Sunday Mass for Catholics. In 1802 he came to Ayr, doing pastoral work among a congregation of 'poor Irish from whom I receive hardly anything.' The directors of Ayr Academy then as later were prepared to ignore the traditional requirement that teachers must be members of the Church of Scotland, and appointed this Roman Catholic priest to the post of French master. Their choice was a wise one. Later in a testimonial the Rector, the Provost, and the Parish Minister together acknowledged that 'he was a faithful and diligent teacher. He always maintained an irreproachable character and was respected by all who had the pleasure of being acquainted with him.' His classes were popular enough to bring him welcome emoluments from fees, so that he could deposit well over a thousand pounds in the Ayr branch of the Bank of Scotland. The problem of religious differences intruded itself on one occasion. A Portuguese gentleman with an Irish wife sent his son to Ayr Academy, to lodge with the Rector after an assurance that the Abbe Nicolas would look after the boy's religious welfare. It is not known how the rector solved the dilemma of requiring a fine from any pupil who did not attend church each Sunday. In 1810 Nicolas resigned to set up as a private teacher of French and Italian in Glasgow, but he continued to minister to the congregations both in Paisley and in Ayr. In 1814 he travelled down to Ayr specially at the request of Private John McManus of the 27th Regiment of Foot, condemned to death for murder. Following the abdication of Napoleon, Nicolas contemplated a return to France, to meet again in Liseux his ageing father, his three sisters, and a brother now invalided out of the army. But sudden illness overtook him and he died in Glasgow late in 1814. He was followed at Ayr Academy by Solomon Gross (1811–38). Thereafter French and Italian were taught by the rector, but with successive foreign assistants who added German to the curriculum. From 1845 for three years there was Edward Trscinski (known as Mr Transky). Then he resigned to return after sixteen years of exile to his native Poland with 'hopes of his country's freedom.' He was followed by a Mr Jacubowski. The post of Modern Languages master was restored in 1854 and held by Thomas Cree (known as 'Pussy') till he retired because of bad health in 1873. Thereafter another Frenchman, Henri Gausseron, inevitably known to the boys as 'Gussie.' He was an emigre, but his command of English was limited, and he proved unsatisfactory, being replaced by Duncan MacKay.

The first two rectors of Ayr Academy had each a brief stay before going off to occupy university chairs: Dr William Meikleham (1796—99) and Thomas Jackson (1799—1809). David Ballingal, the Mathematics master, was then promoted. His term of office (1809—24) was cut short for a less reputable reason. Becoming concerned in some fraudulent transaction which involved him in bankruptcy, the case went to the Court of Session, and he was dismissed. John Smythe Memes, LL.D., who followed was a colourful and influential holder of the office.

DR MEMES
Dr Memes came from Brechin, and early distinguished himself as a student at Aberdeen taking Latin, Greek, and Divinity classes, to which he added Mathematics, Natural Philosophy, and Chemistry, as well as Botany and Anatomy. Employed thereafter as a tutor, he travelled during 1821 and the next two years on the Continent, acquiring fluency in French, Italian, and German, and picking up a knowledge of several unspecified oriental languages. He lectured to the Philosophical Society of London, contributed to the proceedings of the Astronomical Society, and interested himself also in literature and art. This 'gentleman of varied and elegant accomplishments' took over as rector of Ayr Academy in February 1826 just after his 31st birthday.

Dr Memes flung himself into the work with enthusiasm. He took over classes in Mathematics, Natural Philosophy, and Geography. He added History, Botany, and English Composition with Rhetoric and Logic. He applied his skills as a draughtsman to preparing a series of large wall maps for his geography classes. He persuaded the directors to erect scaffolding so that he could personally paint two large terrestrial spheres on the ceiling of the school hall. In 1837 he introduced geographical 'excursions into the country.' To extend the study of Natural History he acquired botanical specimens and created a Botanical garden. He inspired the pupils of his senior English class to original composition and in 1828 and 1829 had printed two small collections of their poems.

When in 1838 the Classics and Modern Language post became vacant he convinced the directors that the remaining masters could easily cope if they 'devote their **individual** attention to their classes.' In the reorganized timetable, he restricted himself to Geography and the 'Ancient and Modern Languages.' In Latin and Greek he introduced the new 'Oxford pronunciation.' In the summer of 1840 he spent six weeks in Paris, visiting six colleges, twenty four municipal schools, the military academy, and a college of education, 'to acquire the most perfect methods of teaching the French language.'

Dr Memes

Several of his colleagues at the academy testified that 'he has discharged the general duties of superintendence with much discretion and punctuality, that an uninterrupted harmony has existed between him and his colleagues.' Another admirer remarked that as well as taking the senior classes, Dr Memes had also taught the 'lowest in the first formation of their letters.' There was further praise. 'His mode of communicating instruction, and managing his classes, is simple and pleasing, and never fails not only to attach his scholars to him personally, but also to make them take a lively interest in the pursuits in which they are engaged.'

His enormous energies were recalled by pupils. 'A simple incident may convey some idea of the intense application and earnest zeal with which Mr Memes laboured for the improvement of all his pupils. We have seen him meet his classes at extra hours, so early as six a.m., teach for twelve hours with trifling intervals — sketch large maps for his Geographical classes till eight at night — meet the Library society at that hour — superintend all their arrangements — direct their views — solve their difficulties, and sum up their debate to the admiration of all, and dismiss them between ten and eleven at night. Next morning, at four or five o'clock, he was to be found actively engaged with his Mathematics class, making plans of the Town Harbour, to be exhibited at the annual examination.'

Meantime he was producing books on a variety of subjects: **A Memoir of Canova and Modern Sculpture** (1828) and **A History of Sculpture, Painting and Architecture** (1837); the **Works of William Cowper** (1834) and a **Life of Cowper** (1837); the **Memoirs of Josephine** (1832) and a translation of the **Memoirs of Bonaparte** (1836); with one of the earliest books on photography, **Daguerre's History and Practice of Photogenic Drawing** (1839).

Dr Memes became recognised and respected in Ayr. A local minister praised him as 'one of the readiest extempore speakers we have seen' and a colleague confirmed that his 'elegance of style in composition' was equalled by 'an eloquence in public speaking which has often enraptured his hearers.' He conducted evening classes in astronomy, and to the Ayr Mechanics' Institute he gave gratuitous instruction. When he delivered a series of Sunday evening lectures on the

Evidences of Christianity in Wallacetown Chapel, all nine hundred seats were occupied, and other people had to be turned away.

The polymathic powers of Dr Memes were widely appreciated. He provided evidence to be presented in parliament on behalf of the Glasgow and Ayr railway company. His knowledge of anatomy was recognised by the Ayrshire Medico-Chirurgical Association. With a party of senior pupils he made a survey and prepared a report on the feasibility of bringing piped water from Carrick Hill into Ayr — for which he was rewarded with a public dinner in his honour. He assisted the Sheriff of Ayr by calculating the trajectory of a bullet from an air gun. When Ayr Town Hall was struck by lightning in January 1838 Memes 'quieted public alarm' and earned the gratitude of the town council by climbing the steeple and assessing that the structure was safe.

Under his rectorship the academy achieved 'steady and progressive prosperity.' Numbers rose from 420 before his arrival in 1826, to a peak of 594 in 1829. In that year he was offered the post of Principal of Dalhousie College, Halifax, Nova Scotia. But this did not materialise. Other disappointments followed. He narrowly failed to be appointed professor of Logic at Edinburgh University in 1836. He was similarly unsuccessful in his application to become Professor of Natural Philosophy at St Andrews in 1837. Left a widower with two sons soon after his coming to Ayr, he had married again in 1834 and had another two sons and a daughter. Then his second wife died.

The roll of the academy declined steadily throughout the thirties till it was less than 400. This was attributed to the outbreak of cholera in Ayr in 1832 and the disappearance of most of the boarders who came to be educated here, some lodging with the rector. Certainly the energies of Memes were flagging. One pupil recalled the senior class in Geography which was held daily in the hour before the lunch interval. Dr Memes used to have brought in to sustain him a glass of wine and a biscuit. After taking these, he would drop off to sleep.

Dr Memes left in 1844 to become minister of the second charge in Hamilton parish church. There he married for a third time, and died in 1858, aged 63.

LAWS TO BE OBSERVED

BY THE

STUDENTS ATTENDING AYR ACADEMY.

I. Diligence and application are most strictly enjoined on all the Students, both in the Academy, and in preparing Lessons at home.

II. No Student is to be absent from any Class, without the knowledge and permission of a Parent or Guardian, intimated to the Master, either in writing or by a satisfactory message.

III. Every Student is required to attend the Public Meetings on Saturday mornings, in the Common Hall, for Prayers and other Duties connected with the general discipline of the Institution. No exemption can be obtained except from the Rector, and if Parents find it necessary unexpectedly to detain their children, a note to that effect will be required on the following Saturday.

IV. Any Student found to have damaged the buildings or property of the Academy must repair the injury; and if the offence shall have been intentionally committed, his conduct will be further subjected to a public investigation.

V. In their behaviour to each other, the Students are to be kind and obliging. All quarrelling, fighting, calling names, and irritating language, are most strictly prohibited. The Senior Students are particularly cautioned against oppressing the Junior Pupils; no one is to injure another's property; and all are required to be most careful of their own books, and those of their fellow Students.

VI. All dangerous amusements are forbidden in general; going into boats, and having or using gunpowder, are most especially prohibited.

VII. The conduct of Students attending so respectable a Seminary should be exemplary: all improper behaviour, therefore, in or out of School; all annoyance to the public by throwing stones or otherwise; all unbecoming language, and insolence offered to any individual, are prohibited in the strongest terms. Neglect of this or any other Law, will subject the offender to all the consequences of an Academical Enquiry.

₊ The co-operation of Parents is earnestly requested in maintaining the observance of these Regulations so obviously calculated for the safety, and the moral as well as literary training of the youth attending the Academy. All concerned are respectfully reminded, that in every learned profession, before entering the Universities, or engaging in any respectable occupation, a Certificate of good behaviour and acquirements will be found useful in every case, and in many instances is indispensable to the future progress of those who have studied at the Academy.

THE BEGINNINGS OF CHANGE

Robert McMillan of Dumfries Academy was appointed, but he died before taking office. The next rector was Dr William Hunter who had previously taught in Campbeltown, Glasgow's 'Andersonian University', Paisley, and Liverpool. Dr Hunter (1844—62) was a man of 'great amiability' and 'ripe scholarship.' He had written an **Anglo Saxon Grammar** (1832), **Symbolica Classica** (1833), and added a **Latin Grammar** (1845) and a **Theory and Practice of Composition** (1857). But his health was poor and he died in office.

In 1852 during Dr Hunter's rectorship a more elaborate scheme of prize awards was instiuted. In that year a former pupil, son of a provost of Ayr, now elevated to the bench as Lord Cowan, donated £60 the interest of which should provide a Cowan Gold Medal for the best pupil each year. At the same time a Mr Hamilton of Hillerhust provided for five Hamilton Silver Medals in English, Classics, Mathematics, Modern Languages, and Writing. And medals were also instituted for Scripture Knowledge. The teachers continued to provide from their own pockets the money for book prizes. And a long-established tradition was continued by the institution in 1855 of a Provost's Prize for Mental Arithmetic.

James MacDonald from Elgin was another notable rector. He sported a bristly moustache and whiskers, he was renowned for his frequent absent-minded mutterings in class, and was known as 'the Grizzly Bear.' But during his term (1862—1883) some quite revolutionary changes in the character of the academy were made.

Dr MacDonald introduced a modern-style time table and planned curriculum. Sports were introduced as an extra-curricular activity. We hear for the first time in 1878 of a tuck-shop 'at Mr Whiteside's shop' opposite the academy. After 1873 control passed from the Board of Directors to the new Ayr Burgh School Board. And in 1880 there was a move into the new building.

Under the management of the directors (1796—1873) the academy enjoyed a 'career of almost uninterrupted popularity and usefulness.' During this period the county town was enjoying continued expansion. Trade and traffic were facilitated by the system of turnpike roads constructed in the later 18th century, later augmented by the railways. In 1840 the Glasgow-Ayr railway brought trains as far as the north harbour. After 1847 there was a link with Kilmarnock. The line was extended into the royal burgh and the present station opened in 1857. Connections were made with Girvan (1860) and Stranraer (1876). Branches from Dalmellington (1856) and Cumnock (1872) brought coal down to the harbour for export. North of the river Newton-upon-Ayr expanded as an industrial area. South of the old royal burgh new residential developments extended towards the race course and to Alloway. In 1873 the royal burgh of Ayr widened its boundaries to swallow the old separate burgh of Newton-upon-Ayr, take in parts of the landward area and Wallacetown in St Quivox parish, and by 1881 contained 24,000 inhabitants. The old town council controlled by some 220 burgesses was reformed in 1833. Annual elections, opened to a widening range of householders, made possible the development of local social services.

While the academy had been instituted in 1796 as a successor to the old burgh school, it was soon clear that one school alone could not cope with the educational needs of this growing community. This was tacitly recognised when the town council approved the continuation of the Wallace Tower-Fish Cross school. When parliament in 1833 authorised grants for providing elementary education this was followed locally by the setting up of new schools under various auspices. Alloway school (1863) and Ayr Grammar school (1868) were sponsored by parents who sought lower fees than at the academy. Smith's Institution (1825), Lady Jane Hamilton's school (1842) and the Carrick Street school (c.1855) were charity schools with very low fees, and free places for poor children. Similarly across the river Newton town council replaced its school at the church (1802) by another elementary school cheekily called Newton Academy (1846). In Wallacetown there was an elementary school in Cross Street and for a time a private Wallacetown Academy. Other elementary schools were provided by various religious bodies. The Free Church (after 1843) took over the Fish Cross school and set up Main Street school in Newton and Weaver Street school in Wallacetown. There was a Roman Catholic school in Elba Street and an Episcopal school in Fullarton Street.

47

Ayr Academy.

TABLE OF FEES.

THE FEES are Payable on the last Saturday of each Quarter, of about Eleven weeks, according to the following Scale:—

ENGLISH DEPARTMENT.

	YEAR OF COURSE.	PER QR.
Reading and Spelling, ...	1st and 2nd,	5s. 0d.
Do. do. with Geography, ...	3rd,	6s. 0d.
Do. do. do. and Elements of Grammar,	4th,	8s. 6d.
Reading, Grammar, and Elements of Composition, 1 hour, ...	5th, 6th, and 7th,	7s. 6d.
Geography, History, and Writing to Dictation, 1 hour, ...	5th, 6th, and 7th,	7s. 6d.
English Language, Composition, and Literature, ...	Advanced Classes,	12s. 6d.

CLASSICAL DEPARTMENT.

Latin, ...	7s. 6d.
Greek, ...	7s. 6d.
Latin and Greek together,, ...	12s. 6d.

MATHEMATICAL DEPARTMENT.

Arithmetic, Junior, ...	5s. 0d.
Do. Senior, including Algebra, ...	6s. 6d.
Do. do. and Elementary Geometry, ...	8s. 6d.
Mathematics, including Geometry, Mechanics, Trigonometry, Calculus, &c. ; and Experimental Physics, ...	10s. 0d.
Navigation, ...	10s. 0d.

WRITING AND DRAWING DEPARTMENT.

Writing, ...	5s. 0d.
Elementary (Freehand) Drawing, ...	7s. 6d.
Drawing (Mechanical, Landscape, &c.), ...	12s. 6d.
Book-keeping, ...	7s. 6d.

Pupils who take Drawing on alternate days with Writing are charged for both the corresponding Drawing Fee, except Beginners, who are charged 6s. 6d. Pupils who take two hours of Writing are charged 2s. extra.

MODERN LANGUAGES.

French, ...	10s. 6d.
German, ...	15s. 0d.
French and German, in one hour, ...	13s. 6d.
German, two hours a week, ...	7s. 6d.

Matriculation Fee, 2s. 6d. per Session.

The School Hours extend from 9 a.m. to 3 p.m., with suitable intervals.

Ayr Academy with its relatively high fees was now catering for only a small proportion of the younger children of the town and had, according to an official report of 1868, a 'genuine middle class population.' Nearly fifty per cent were 'children of shopkeepers and clerks.' There were some of higher social class, including scholars from other parts of Ayrshire and beyond, but now only eight 'children of landed proprietors.' At the other end of the scale there were a dozen free scholars. These were maintained by the bequests of Fergusson of Doonholm (1794) and Hamilton of Pinmore (1829). But altogether there was only a score of 'children of artisans, labourers, etc.' The number of girls in the school was never high. In 1829 there were 226, falling to 48 in 1837 and rising again thereafter. The 1868 figure was typical — 120 girls forming just about a third of the total roll of 362. While better-off boys went to the academy, many of their

Ayr, 13th Oct. 1831.

Sir,

In consequence of finding very great inconvenience from the use of candles in conducting the business of my classes, in the Academy during the winter months, I beg, through you, to submit to the Directors, for their consideration, whether it might not be proper for them to introduce Gas into the Institution. As the main gaspipe is already at the Academy gates, I would think that the expense for bringing a branch of it into the lower part of the building, would not be much, whereas, by its introduction the benefit to the students would be great.

I am, Sir,
Very Respectfully,
Yr. Obt. St.

J. Ridley.

To the Chairman of the
Directors of Ayr Academy

sisters were sent to local private schools for young ladies. In any case, that girls had to be taught in separate classes could be something of a nuisance.

Some pupils of this era — local boys and incomers — made more than a local reputation in later life. There were three judges: John Cowan (1789—1878) who as Lord Cowan donated the Cowan Gold Medal; James Crawford (1805—1876) who became Lord Ardmillan; William Hunter, later Lord Hunter. There were two minor authors: Hew Ainslie (1792—1878) and Andrew Kennedy Hutchison Boyd (1825—99) who wrote as 'AKHB.' There were two men of action: Admiral Sir John Ross (1777—56), the Arctic explorer, and General James George Smith Neill (1810—57), a hero of the Indian Mutiny whose statue stands in Wellington Square.

Sir John Ross in the Arctic.

Yet despite the achievements of the academy, there were difficulties. Finances were barely adequate. The original subscriptions provided the building. But there was not enough to build a house for the rector as was hoped. A janitor's house was long delayed. An often promised library never materialised. When gas mains were laid along Fort Street in 1831 and Mr Ridley pointed out that it would provide so much better illumination for his English classes than candles, it was agreed to instal gas, provided the teacher paid the cost from his fees.

The bequests of Fergusson of Doonholm and Hamilton of Pinmore plus the annual £100 from the town council provided basic payments for the rectors and masters. But fees formed the main portion of their remuneration. As a result, the masters whenever they could annexed subjects to their own department, and might suffer when a new rector arrived and made his own choice of classes. Thus for a long period the Mathematics master had little more than arithmetic and book-keeping to cope with. So in 1838 Dr Memes easily persuaded the directors — and other masters — to share out the work of six among four. There was an additional difficulty. A master who enrolled a large number of pupils had to decide whether to try and teach them all himself, or with the permission of the directors employ an assistant at his own expense.

As a result of all this, the masters had to spend a great deal of their time on elementary work which was more remunerative. In 1850, a typical year, more than half the enrolments were for such junior classes. Reading had 123 enrolments (84 boys, 39 girls), Writing had 117 (85, 32), Arithmetic had 136 (72, 64). Senior classes attracted fewer enrolments. English Composition had 60 (46,14); Geography had a continuing popularity with 72 (54,18); Drawing had only 23 (15,8). There were classes with boys only in Maths (20), Greek (24), Latin (26), and Book-keeping (29), Modern Languages never attracted many pupils. French had only 26 (13,13) and 4 boys took German. Italian had lapsed. History introduced in 1819 failed to become established; nor did Botany survive for more than a few years after 1826. In particular, the original high hopes of developing the teaching of science had not been realised. In 1818 only four pupils were taking Natural Philosophy and seven taking Chemistry. In 1834 comparable numbers were ten and eight. Thereafter the sciences lapsed, and an attempt to re-establish them in 1865 proved unsuccessful.

DR MACDONALD'S NEW CURRICULUM
To remedy some of these difficulties Dr MacDonald almost as soon as he arrived in 1862 began, with the approval of the directors, to plan a completely new curriculum. The prospectus for the session 1877/78 reveals just what a transformation was accomplished.

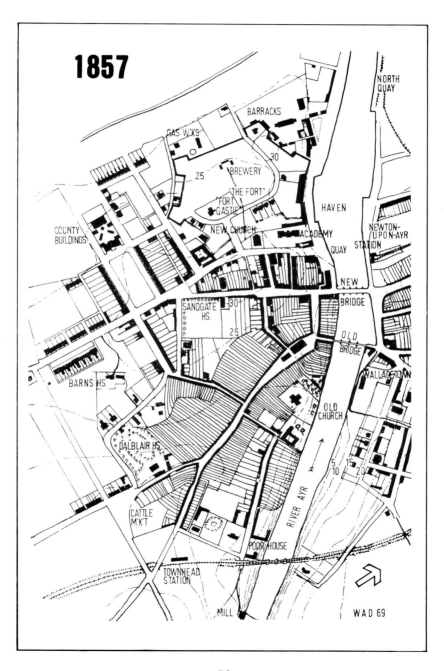

1857

NORTH QUAY

BARRACKS

GAS W'KS

30

25 BREWERY

'THE FORT'

FORT CASTLE

HAVEN

COUNTY BUILDINGS

NEW CHURCH

ACADEMY

NEWTON-UPON-AYR STATION

QUAY

NEW

BRIDGE

SANDGATE HS.

30

25

OLD BRIDGE

BARNS HS.

WALLACETOWN

OLD CHURCH

DALBLAIR HS.

5 15
10 20

CATTLE M'KT

RIVER AYR

POOR HOUSE

TOWNHEAD STATION

MILL

WAD 69

53

There were now five preparatory classes catering for children between the ages of six and ten. In the Higher school, pupils continued on a common course for two years in the Junior division, then for their final three or four years in the Senior division might opt either for the Classical or Modern section. No longer was a scholar enrolled for certain classes only, but for a year's course. Charges ranged from 7/6 to £1/12/6 per quarter in the preparatory classes, and from £2 to £2/15/- in the Higher school. In addition there was a continued charge of a few pence for a matriculation ticket, introduced in 1846 to replace the traditional Candlemas offerings which paid for coals and cleaning of the school.

All pupils (except the youngest) now followed a daily time table with six periods from 9 a.m. till 3 p.m. Prep. Class 1 took reading and spelling only; to which were added in Class 2, writing; Class 3, Arithmetic and Geography; Class 4, Grammar and Drawing; Class 5, History and elementary Latin.

In the Higher school all pupils in Classes 1 and 2 took English, History, Geography, Latin, French, Arithmetic, Writing and Drawing, and Geometry added in Class 2. Thereafter all continued with English, Latin, French, German, Arithmetic, and more advanced Maths. The Classical section had also Greek; the Modern section could take bookkeeping, drawing, and science, and some might drop Latin.

The prospectus added that 'The Moral and Religious training of the Pupils is carefully attended to. The Scriptures are read in all the Junior Classes, while the Senior Classes either read the Greek Testament or receive lessons from some portion of Scripture History.' A non-denominational protestantism was presented by the rector (who belonged to the Free Church), the Writing master (U.P. Church), and the Mathematics and Modern Language masters (who were members of the established Church of Scotland).

The roll of the academy had declined from a maximum of nearly 600 under Dr Memes to just under 300; had risen again for a time in Dr Hunter's earlier years; now under Dr MacDonald's new regime numbers quickly grew from 320 to more than 400. More important, the proportion in the Higher school was augmented. In 1874 there were 54 scholars under nine years, 49 between nine and twelve, and no fewer than

316 older than that. All but 15 of the under-twelves were from Ayr, but of the others, 102 local boys and 63 local girls were joined by 113 boys and 38 girls who travelled daily by train, or lodged in Ayr. Both the rector and the Mathematics master took boarders. This was now more than before a county academy. Elsewhere in Ayrshire, Kilmarnock (1807), Irvine (1813), and Speirs School, Beith (1888) offered more limited opportunities and their combined rolls were smaller than that of Ayr Academy.

Assistant English Master—Ayr Academy.
JULY, 1871.

PARTICULARS OF APPOINTMENT.

1.—DUTIES.—To teach, under the superintendence of the Rector, and with such assistance as he may deem necessary, the first six English classes, embracing Reading, Spelling, Dictation, Geography, History, and Grammar. The course of study, classification of pupils, and exercise of discipline, are regulated by the Rector, so as to harmonise with the system followed in the classes taught by him.

2.—EMOLUMENTS.—To receive out of the fees of these six classes, after payment of retiring allowance to a former teacher and the cost of additional assistance (the assistant to be provided by the Rector), as well as any other necessary outlay, a fixed salary of £100 and one-third of the remaining surplus. On the average of the last two years, the sum available, after payment of retiring allowance and other deductions mentioned above, may be expected to amount to about £145. Allocated as proposed, this would yield an income of say £115 to the assistant teacher ; but no guarantee can be given, as the sum may increase or diminish according to circumstances,—in particular, in proportion to the exertions of the teacher.

3.—TENURE.—The appointment will be made by the Rector, subject to the approval of the Directors. It will be terminable by two months' notice given on either side any time after four months of a Session has passed.

4.—QUALIFICATIONS.—Candidates, besides producing satisfactory testimonials as to character and attainments, must have had considerable experience in teaching English to junior as well as to more advanced classes. Preference will be given to a well-educated young man who intends to make teaching his profession.

5.—TIME.—Candidates must lodge two copies of their Testimonials with Mr W. F. M'CUBBIN, Solicitor, Sandgate Street, Ayr, on or before the 24th inst.; and the successful applicant will be required to enter on his duties on 22d August.

THE SCHOOL BOARD TAKES CONTROL

The Education (Scotland) Act of 1872 set up elected school boards which could take over existing schools and levy a local rate for educational purposes. All children between the ages of five and thirteen must be provided for, and attendance was made compulsory. From 1873 the new Ayr Burgh School Board became responsible for the management of the academy. Wisely the Board decided that 'should any alteration be deemed advisable, it should be done with considerable caution.'

A Class Group in 1873.

The Directors of the Academy continued in existence till 1890. Though they no longer managed the school, they retained control of its various endowments. As recently as 1868 David Cowan of Auchendrane had bequeathed £2000 to provide a bursary for academy pupils going on to Glasgow or Edinburgh university. In the same year two Patrick bursaries and Edinburgh-Ayrshire Club bursaries provided further opportunities for students going to Edinburgh. For Glasgow university there were various Ayrshire bursaries possibly available. The selection of the Cowan and Patrick bursars was made by the Directors till the establishment of an Ayr Education Trust in 1890 made the continued existence of an Academy Board of Directors unnecessary.

More complicated was the Board of Directors' role in making payments towards the rector's and masters' salaries from the Doonholm and Pinmore funds. The School Board tried to disentangle details of the various contracts made by the directors with the several masters and assistants. They also realized that the allocation of money from fees required to be regularised. When course fees replaced class fees in 1876, arrangements were made for a more systematic plan of remuneration. Fixed annual sums were allocated to the rector, each master, and the assistants. If the new curriculum prospered, any surplus in fees would be divided proportionally, 'so that each teacher is equally interested in the prosperity, not of his own section of the Academy, but of the whole'.

One further innovation was made by the School Board. The school had once been inspected by representatives of the church, and latterly in an erratic manner by the directors. Instead of taking this traditional responsibility on their own shoulders, the Board decided to engage annually external examiners who could authoritatively report on the academy's standards. In 1874 a first invitation went to Mr James Donaldson of the Edinburgh Royal High School, and Mr William Jack, editor of the Glasgow Herald. After 1886 the services of Her Majesty's Inspectors would be provided by what was then entitled the Scotch Education Department.

Ayr Burgh School Board had, however, a wider area of supervision. They were busy with their major task of providing elementary schooling for all the town's younger children. A massive school building programme was begun, replacing the old schools and building new ones: Newtonhead (1874) replaced Main Street and Weaver Street schools; Wallacetown (1875); Holmston (1884) replaced Smith's Institution; Alloway (1896); Grammar School (1909); Newton Academy (1911). Lady Jane Hamilton's school was extended. The High Street and Carrick Street schools were closed. New schools were opened at Russell Street (1890) and Newton Park (1905). Outwith the Board's control, St Margaret's R.C. school was opened in 1893, and the Episcopal school continued in Fullarton Street till 1907.

By an anomaly in the parliamentary legislation, no provision could be made for maintaining or replacing a 'higher class school' like Ayr Academy which provided post-elementary instruction. Nevertheless the School Board explored the possibility of raising another public subscription, and ultimately resolved to build a new academy at the expense of the local rates. Such a new building was urgently needed. Both fabric and furniture were obsolete. Whenever enrolments increased there had been overcrowding. As early as 1828 it had been noted as less than satisfactory that 170 pupils had to be accommodated in one of the smaller rooms.

Once a decision was made to rebuild, the next question was where. A site was considered at the corner of Fort Street and Charlotte Street. There in 1876 Templeton's carpet works had been burned down. James A. Morris, architect and former pupil, argued strongly for the modernisation of the old academy. The final decision was for a new academy just in front of the existing building.

THE FOURTH SCHOOL: SINCE 1880
THE NEW ACADEMY

At noon on Tuesday 31st August 1880 there was an all-male gathering of one hundred guests for the formal opening of the new academy. There was 'a service of cake and wine' followed by 'a few toasts' to celebrate 'the beginning of a new period of enlarged success.'

The building, of white sandstone from Ravenscraig quarry, had been designed by Messrs Clarke and Bell of Glasgow at a cost of £9000. The hundred and forty feet front was of 'a more ornamental character,' with a central portico of Corinthian style. Above the doorway were the sculptured heads of Watt, Burns, and Wilkie, representing Science, Literature, and Art.

The Ayr Academy, 1895.

Inside was accommodation for the various departments, still almost separately managed. On the ground floor left was English. On the other side, the Writing Room and Studio. There was the Board Room and a Gentlemen's Staff Room. Upstairs were the Mathematics, Classics, and smaller Modern Language departments, with the Rector's room and one for the new Lady Superintendent.

The Frontage, with heads of Watt, Burns and Wilkie.

There had been one awkward planning problem. The install-
ation of hot water pipes for heating and gas brackets for
lighting was complicated enough. The major difficulty was
arranging to keep the boys and girls segregated. Until the last
years of the old academy this had been done by having
separate classes for Young Ladies. The School Board agreed
that 'it is a good thing for boys and girls to compete together
in class work; but otherwise it is desirable they should be
separated.' In the new academy, boys were to enter by the
central door at the front, and girls at the rear. Each classroom
had separate doors for boys and girls. Their paths must never
meet, even at the top of the stairs. The Scotch Education
Department insisted on this. In a letter from Whitehall they
ordered the plans to be altered: 'The securing of arrangements necessary for ordinary decency is a matter of more
grave importance than any deterioration of the appearance of
the staircase.' Also, the Board appointed as Matron or Lady
Superintendent Mrs Jessie Craigie at £80 a year, to 'look after
the manners and conduct of the girls.' There were girls' and
boys' playgrounds, separated at the back by a high wall and
at the front by railings, to be supervised respectively by the
Lady Superintendent and by the janitor.

A PERIOD OF EXPANSION
The rectorship was taken over quite soon by William Maybin,
after the appointment of Dr MacDonald to Kelvinside.
Maybin came here (1883 —1910) after a spell as rector of
Paisley grammar school and academy. An Ulsterman by birth,
he was a tall, robust, and vigorous figure with greying reddish

60

hair and a full beard. He was a commanding personality in his frock coat and black silk hat. Yet 'the Billy' had a kindly nature, generously nurturing the genius of George Douglas Brown, as will later be shown.

William Maybin

Under Maybin's rectorship at the turn of the century the academy expanded its curriculum in various novel ways. The period can be graphically recreated from numerous reminiscences, now supplemented by photographs. There is also a series of official reports on the work of the academy by H.M. Inspectors from the Scotch Education Department, covering the years from 1887 till 1910.

James Thomson who was the Mathematics master (1868—1901) was a distinguished character, long remembered as 'Dandy Jim.' He was prim and trig, with a waistline reputedly encircled by a corset. He wore a large jewelled tiepin and coloured waistcoat, and on his watch chain was a miniature gun, since he was a keen volunteer artilleryman. In his coat tail pocket he carried his strap along with a large coloured handkerchief. He was slow and deliberate both in step and speech. Pupils described him as 'fatherly' and 'warm hearted' but nevertheless 'no boy would dare to take a liberty.' He had been to university, but had never graduated. This was not uncommon with masters appointed in the days of the old academy. The Board of Directors had no official regulations to limit their choice. After Thomson had to resign because of ill health, the Board appointed Hugh Jamieson as his successor. By this time not only professional qualification but also teacher training was required. But Jamieson in manner was of the old school, tall and thin, with a stern and eagle eye, and a voice like thunder.

Laurence Anderson, who developed the teaching of Art in the Studio behind the Writing Room, was sometimes remembered because he did not use the tawse. 'Pluto' preferred a cane, and one noted as having a particularly 'stinging effect.' The S.E.D. report of 1887 commended the 'striking excellence of the work' in the Art department, which was in a 'most flourishing condition.' In particular they remarked on an exhibition of drawing by pupils which 'excelled anything of the kind I had ever seen before.' Anderson's long term (1858—1902) following the even-longer tenure by his predecessor, Robert Taylor, meant that between them they spanned three centuries from the 18th to the 20th. After his retiral he maintained his interest in the academy till he died in 1923 in his 90th year. His successor, R. Smeaton Douglas (1902— 1912), had alas a span of only ten years before death cut short a brilliant career. Personally he was regarded as kindly, generous, goodhearted, and likeable. Professionally he was an able portraitist. As a teacher of Art he was commended in S.E.D. reports by F.H. Newbery for his innovations in craft work — embroidery, stencilling, metal work, stained glass and for his lectures on furniture design.

The English master was William Cormack (1877—1895). S.E.D. reports of 1887 and 1888 note his 'acknowledged capacity as an excellent teacher.' He was attempting dramatic work with Class 2, which contained 25 boys and 20 girls: 'A short scene from Hamlet was taken by some of the boys and acted very well.' George Liddell who followed him had to resign after only two years. Through ill health he had to go off to 'the high Alps.' William Dick in 1897 began his long association with the academy. He was assessed as 'an unusually capable and thoughtful teacher' of English and History, despite his slight speech impediment, and well liked for his quiet sense of humour. Though a strict disciplinarian, his soft pigskin strap was accounted a joke. He was tall, dark, and well-groomed.

The Modern Languages department, teaching French and German, was for a long and notable period under Duncan MacKay (1880—1914). Like the others attired in a tile hat and frock coat, yet this tall angular figure with lofty brow and bushy side whiskers, always hurrying despite a slight limp, appeared a sort of Dickensian character. 'Old Rusty' was highly respected, and so was his black and ugly strap which was considered the sorest known. Successive S.E.D. reports were full of praise for 'the spirited and sympathetic way in which he manages his classes.' They noted that 'Mr MacKay has developed his new method of teaching . . . the results are remarkable.' He had introduced 'the direct method' and indeed wrote some textbooks. He obtained from Vienna and Paris specially prepared pictures to use in his oral work. And, as 'an interesting and useful novelty' he enthusiastically taught the singing of simple French songs.

Duncan MacKay

The new academy was attracting also assistants of high calibre, some of whom were specially remembered: A.J. Thomson, 'Wee Tommy', a skilled artist and penman; 'Sandy' Cormack, son of the former English master, who created a sensation with his knickerbocker suit; Alexander Alexander, 'Double Sandy', who taught English and Mathematics, and was an enthusiastic botanist and geologist; 'Froggy' Mansard, one of a series of foreign assistants.

The academy was also extending its curriculum, and appointing teachers who could not appropriately be attached to any of the traditional departments. Sewing and knitting were taught in what was called 'the Industrial department' by the Lady Superintendent, Mrs Jessie Craigie (1880–1906), followed by Miss Kate Richardson (1906–1918). In 1891 a class in Shorthand was introduced. James McGeachie was appointed as part-time teacher, and attached to the Art department, which was also responsible for Book-keeping, that consistently popular subject. Also in 1895 a significant step was taken in appointing Miss Margaret Buchanan as Infants Mistress, a post she held for 28 years. In 1900 she had a class of 40 pupils and was giving them 'kindly and efficient training in which Musical Drill and Kindergarten work find due place.' In 1906 she acquired the first of several assistants. Thereafter the senior masters were able to shed their traditional responsibility for teaching the younger pupils, no doubt gratefully. Then, by another change, the long-distant tradition of a 'sang schule' was re-established. In 1895 it was agreed that Miss Margaret Ramsay might begin piano lessons for those pupils who were prepared to pay her fees. In 1906 Frederick Ely was similarly appointed to teach singing, and in due course he made this an integral part of the class time-tables. Other innovations followed. In 1897 the first Gymnastics master was appointed, associated with the new interest in sports, later looked at in detail. In 1907 Ewan Ritchie was appointed as Manual Instructor to teach wood-work.

One omission had to be dealt with. The 'want of Education in the Sciences' was still being complained of in 1881. A year later Robert McMillan was appointed to the Mathematics department as a specialist assistant who would create in due course a new and separate Science department, established in 1896. Despite initial difficulties of 'very meagre equipment,' McMillan who was 'an admirable teacher' achieved 'remarkable success.' He was teaching electricity and magnetism, and by 1904 was making 'occasional excursions into wireless telegraphy.' Once a chemistry laboratory became available, his experimental work was most popular with the boys.

Though the new academy opened in 1880 had been accounted able to accommodate far more that the 420 pupils on the roll, expansion into specialised areas required extended facilities. The School Board could hardly make any further call on the ratepayers of Ayr. So a three-day bazaar was organised for March 1895. This produced, incidentally, the 'Bazaar Book' which Miss Jane Campbell filled with interesting historical details. Altogether over £900 was raised. This supplemented a new annual grant for 'higher class schools' administered by the County Committee on Secondary Education which had been formed in 1892. A £3000 extension to the rear was designed by James A. Morris, an old boy who had been disappointed not to be chosen as architect for the new building of 1880. This extension of 1895 comprised an Infants room, gymnasium, chemistry laboratory and demonstration room, and a boiler house. Even more elaborate developments followed. In 1906 electricity was installed for lighting. In 1907 Morris was asked to add a separate additional block to the north, with a suite of rooms for art and other practical sujects, at a further cost of £8000. And in 1912 he would design a major reconstruction project.

CLASSROOM STUDIES ABOUT 1900

The course timetables as devised by Dr MacDonald required some modification by Mr Maybin in view of the changes. The school day was extended from six to seven periods. The dinner interval was increased from 20 minutes to 30 minutes and then to one hour. Classes which had finished at 3 p.m. continued till 3.30 and then 4 p.m. The school session ran from September till the end of June. Maybin introduced term exams in October, March and May, continuing the traditional medal examination in June. Some of these changes were inspired by the introduction in 1888 of the Leaving Certificate. This annual external examination was instituted by the Scotch Education Department. In the first year 29 senior pupils sat 109 papers (with only 3 failures) in English, Latin, Greek, French, German, Mathematics and Arithmetic. In 1880 Higher and Lower grades were instituted. By 1896 there had been instituted the group Leaving Certificate, for many years afterwards a recognised qualification, based on a group of four Highers or three Highers plus two Lowers. The imposition of new strict academic standards was extended throughout the school. After passing through what was now known as the Primary department, pupils had to pass a Qualifying examination before admission into the Intermediate department, to which there was an influx of pupils from other primary schools in the town and district. After three years there was an Intermediate Certificate to be gained before a score of pupils advanced into the Secondary department proper. Less than a dozen annually were able to achieve the high standard of a group Leaving Certificate.

Fees varied from around £4 per session in the first classes to around £10 in the highest. A number of free places was provided after competitive examination by the Ayr Educational Trust, by the County Committee on Secondary Education, by the School Board itself, and by bursaries provided for in a bequest from Dr McCosh of Kirkmichael.

That there was opportunity for the poor lad o' pairts in confirmed by the enrolment in 1884 of George Brown, entering the Higher Fourth Class in his fifteenth year. In the Fee Book, the parent's name is given as 'Miss Sarah Gemmell, Dairy, Kayshill, Stair,' and payments were 'Reduced to £1 per quarter by masters.' Maybin generously took under his wing this bright boy whom the schoolmaster of Coylton had recommended to him. His fees were subsidised by

Maybin personally, and indeed he provided him with a holiday in Ireland one summer. Under Maybin's patronage, George took the Scripture Medal in 1886. In the following year he did particularly well, gaining the Hamilton Silver Medal for Classics and the Cowan Bursary which would take him to Glasgow University. By an odd coincidence this was the first year that a detailed report was made on the classes in Ayr Academy by the Scotch Education Department. Unusually, the inspectors named pupils. George Brown was 4th out of seven in a test on English literature, but 1st in the essay. 'These higher English classes are undoubtedly in a high state of efficiency.' He was 2nd out of five in Latin and Greek, 3rd in Greek Testament, 1st in unseen passages in both languages. The inspector, Dr John Birrell, made special comment: 'It has seldom been my good fortune to revise such full and accurate papers as those of Currie and Brown.' As a footnote, in the five mathematical papers, taken by five pupils, he was 2nd, 3rd, 4th, 4th and last in arithmetic. Going on to Glasgow University, he won the Snell Exhibition which took him to Oxford. A subsequent literary career in London was cut short by his untimely death in 1902. Just a year before had been published his now-famous novel, George Douglas Brown's **The House with the Green Shutters,** which he affectionately dedicated to William Maybin.

George Douglas Brown

The establishment of the new academy encouraged others to offer more tangible tokens of respect. The Cowan Gold Medal of 1852 was complemented in 1881 by the Coats Gold Medal for the modern or commercial side, donated by Sir Peter Coats of Auchendrane. There were also added, in 1881 a MacDonald prize for Classics and English, in memory of the late rector; the McCreath medal for Chemistry presented in 1887 by Andrew McCreath, a former pupil settled in Pennsylvania; the Porteous medal for the junior division in 1888; McCowan English and Art prizes, 1906; Grant prizes in French and German, 1909. Other gifts were David McCowan's presentation of books and a bookcase, 1906, which formed the basis of a library; James Morris's oak wall panels on which the names of medallists might be inscribed, 1910. Other friends began a continuing process of donating books, old medals, and other relics of the old school. John Woodburn (1843—1902) who had left the academy in 1858 and became Lieutenant Governor of Bengal in 1898, bequeathed valuable mementoes. Sir Thomas Oliver (1853—1942), an authority on industrial diseases, made the first of several gifts in 1912. In memory of his mother he awarded the Margaret Oliver Memorial Prize in housewifery for pupils at the evening classes (which the School Board had been providing since 1895). Ayr Academy Club of former pupils donated a Silver Cup and badge for the most successful athlete at the school Sports in 1912.

Lord Cowan, Donor of the Gold Medal.

SPORTS

Sports, which came to form an almost essential aspect in the life of the modern school, emerged in an organised form in the 1870s and 1880s. As far back as 1775 we read of handball at the old burgh school. In the early 19th century there were informal races down the Academy Vennel and round the old Tolbooth in the Sandgate, before it was demolished in 1824. High jumping was practised outside the old academy on the grassy part of the playground beside the church.

By the 1860s cricket was popular in Ayr, which had five adult clubs, as well as three junior clubs of which academy boys were members — the Academy Club, Ailsa Club, and Victoria Club. They played on the Low Green, the Racecourse, and Carrick Park by Midton Road. It was the Academy Club which, chancing to choose maroon as its team colours, bequeathed these to the academy itself.

AYR ACADEMY FIRST XV., 1874.
Back Row — A. Lennon; B. Wright; Ch. Brown; Eb. Young; Tom Tosh;
R. Jardine; D. Wilson; J. Muir; J. Watson.
Front Row — A. Semple; R. Brown; M. Shirley; R. Laing; D. Kirkland;
H. Fullarton—Captain.

Football was also played, and when the new craze for what was called association football swept the West of Scotland, the Ayr Academy Football Club in 1872 was undecided as to which code to adopt. When an Ayrshire Football Association was formed in 1877, Ayr Academy was among the score of

AYR ACADEMICAL ATHLETIC CLUB

AMATEUR

ATHLETIC SPORTS,

SPRINGVALE PARK,

SATURDAY. 11th MAY, 1878.

President.

MAJOR R. F. F. CAMPBELL, OF CRAIGIE.

Vice-President.

ROBERT M. POLLOK, Esq., OF MIDDLETON.

Judges.

JAMES THOMSON, Esq | HUGH CLIMIE, Esq.

Starter.

JOHN MURDOCH. Esq.

Stewards.

J. M. M. MORTON, Esq.	DR. KAY.
J. A MORRIS, Esq.	A. W. STRUTHERS, Esq.
WM. CORMACK, Esq.	DR. NAISMYTH.

Committee.

ROBERT MACCALLUM.	DAVID SOMMERVILLE.
WM. HIGHET.	JAMES W. MORRIS.
J. W. YOUNG.	ROBERT S. CLIMIE.
ROBERT PATON.	JOHN MURDOCH.
JOHN MURRAY.	

Clerk of the Course.

JOHN W. YOUNG.

Secretary.

ROBERT S. CLIMIE.

☞ *VISITORS are requested to keep OUTSIDE THE ROPES*

HUGH HENRY, PRINTER.

clubs involved. In the following year Ayr Academicals entered for the Scottish Cup, but they were defeated in the first round by Mauchline. Three pupils of this period went on to become Scottish soccer internationalists: David Allan played for Queens Park; W.W. Beveridge of Glasgow University F.C.; and John Smith of Mauchline who introduced soccer to Edinburgh University, played with Beveridge in the 1879 International against England, and took in all seven international caps. In 1879 Ayr Academicals combined with Ayr Thistle to form Ayr F.C., which itself joined with Ayr Parkhouse in 1910 to form Ayr United. Long before this, within the academy, the devotees of rugby had triumphed. A Rugby XV was playing in 1874. By 1889 regular fixtures were being played with schools in Beith, Greenock and Glasgow.

The first organised Sports Day was held in Springvale Park in 1877, involving senior and former pupils. For the next couple of years it developed as an amateur open meeting. In 1880 began the continuous series of annual School Sports, held on Saturday afternoons in Springvale and later Somerset Park. In the first year there were twenty six events. Some were for under-nines, some for former pupils, all carefully handicapped. There was an egg race, an obstacle race, and a mile-long bicycle race. It concluded with the final tie of a football competition.

Parallel with those extra-mural activities came the introduction of physical education into the academy. In 1889 when a new janitor was appointed it was required that the applicants should be handymen, able to do small repairs, and also 'able to give instruction in drill.' In 1897 a full-time instructor in gymnastics was advertised for, who must be a married man. 'The reason is obvious,' it was noted. One Robert McQueen was appointed, who immediately deserted his wife and absconded. John Farrell (1897—1904) stayed rather longer. He had been assistant gym instructor at Kilmarnock Academy, which was obviously ahead of Ayr in this respect. At first, instruction was optional, and fees had to be paid. Soon it was made compulsory for both boys and girls, made possible by the provision of one gym in 1907 and another in 1912. In 1907 Miss Charlotte Hay was made Instructress in Physical Exercises for Girls, and by 1910 hockey for girls was being played.

WAR

Alexander Emslie (1910—1918) who came from Ellon presided for a short period when there were important changes within the academy and important events outside.

Already before Maybin's death in 1910 plans were afoot for major reorganisation. The Scotch Education Department was complaining that the traditional system of management was obsolete. 'Really six schools housed in one building . . . the control of the Rector is more nominal than real,' they remarked in 1906. Two years later they re-iterated that 'the different departments in the Academy have become much too sharply demarcated . . . the Rector is de facto too exclusively the mere head of the classical department, in the actual teaching of which most of his time is taken up.' In 1910 George Turnbull, already senior assistant, was put in charge of a reconstituted Classical department.

When Emslie was appointed, it was as the academy's first non-teaching rector. The contract specifically insisted that he should 'exercise a general authority over and be responsible for the conduct, management, and discipline of the whole school.' He should visit the departments regularly and hold monthly consultative meetings with the masters. He was 'not expected to do any further teaching than is absolutely necessary. In any event, he shall not teach more than ten periods in the week.' Nor should he take in boarders, as previous rectors were expected to

Alexander Emslie

do. To assist the rector in his administrative work, a typist was appointed. Miss Jane McGill (1910—15) was followed as school secretary by Miss Jenny Morgan (1915—45) and Miss J. Edith R. McGarva (1945—   ).

The 1912 Prospectus shows the academy reorganised on departmental lines. The six masters were in charge of English, History, and Geography; Classics; Mathematics; Modern Languages; Experimental Science; Art. There was a total of fifteen assistant teachers within these departments, plus others responsible for Physical Culture, Domestic Science, Pianoforte and Singing, Commercial Subjects, and Manual Instruction. Needlework was still taught by the Lady Superintendent. There was a separate Primary department with four teachers. 'The members of the Teaching Staff are all either University Graduates with Honours, fully qualified and recognised by the Scotch Education Department . . . or Teachers holding diplomas of recognised Colleges and Central Institutions.'

Outdoor Art Class about 1900.

In 1912 the school building itself underwent massive reconstruction, with James A. Morris in charge of the design. The Art block was directly connected to the main building. This was itself completely redesigned, as the S.E.D. report approvingly noted: 'not, as formerly of a series of separate suites of rooms constituting isolated departments, but of a large central hall surrounded by the various classrooms all opening directly into the corridors.' A new rector's room and small office were formed inside the front entrance. Two new staircases were installed. Further additions were made so that the school now had 26 classrooms; two gymnasia and two laboratories; rooms for typewriting and needlework beside the manual room on the ground floor at the art block; high up on the left, accommodation for cookery, laundry, housewifery, and music; plus a dining room for 70 pupils reached by an iron staircase. Little remained of the 1880 building save the external shell and frontage. At what was now a teachers' entrance on the old front, there still survived in 1982 a rubberised mat inscribed 'Writing Room.' At the back of Room 10 remained the blocked-up window on what had once been the rear wall of the academy.

The Academy showing 1912 extension.

Appropriately, in 1912 Ayr Academy obtained a grant of a coat of arms, thanks to forty three old boys who provided the finance. Certain items on the shield are derived from the arms of the burgh of Ayr: William the Lion's castle beside the sea; the head of John the Baptist, patron of the parish church; the Holy Lamb bearing the banner of Scotland. Added to these is a book of learning inscribed 'Dominus Illuminatio Mea.' and the motto, 'Respice Prospice.' This coat of arms was emblazoned above the new central hall where the school now assembled each morning for prayers.

Visit of Lord Haldane, 11 January 1912.

Already in Maybin's latter years, war had made its first impact on the academy. He was saddened by the loss of nine old boys who died on active service in the Boer War, for whom a memorial was unveiled in 1910. Preparations for another greater war were afoot. In 1909 the government as part of its military preparations instituted an Officers' Training Corps in schools and universities. In 1912 Lord Haldane, Secretary of State for War, on a visit to Ayr inspected the Ayr Academy Cadet Corps. Seventy boys over the age of thirteen were uniformed and drilled. On the outbreak of war in 1914 seven assistant teachers immediately volunteered and were replaced by women on a temporary basis. The strength of the Cadet Corps grew to 130, encouraged by the Rector's prophetic statement that 'the boys on the benches today may be in the trenches tomorrow.' The Academy magazine which had commenced regular publication in 1909 now provided a Roll of Honour in each issue, listing those who had joined up. A special 'Xmas Souvenir to Former Pupils on War Service, 1917' noted over five hundred names. Throughout the war the academy involved itself in fund-raising activities, contributed to war savings, provided comforts and gifts for the troops, made donations to war charities, and maintained 'Ayr Academy beds' in military hospitals. Within the school it was 'business as usual.' Rugby, cricket, hockey, cycling, golf, and swimming clubs still operated, as did the recently formed literary and debating society and the field club.

Cadet Corps in Front Playground.

At length came the end of the war in 1918; a number of boys actually returned from the forces to become pupils again. The cost of the war in lives could be reckoned with the unveiling in the central hall in 1921 of the War Memorial bearing the names of 4 teachers and 111 former pupils who had 'laid down their lives for their country.'

The Cadet Corps continued active throughout the interwar period, and after the outbreak of the Second World War in 1939 made record recruitments. An Air Training Corps also met in the academy and attracted other boys. As before there were fund-raising ventures, a concert party playing to troops stationed in the area, new civil defence duties, and providing for evacuees from Clydeside. Once again many teachers and senior pupils left the classroom for the forces. A second War Memorial bore the names of 78 former pupils who lost their lives in war between 1939 and 1945. The Cadet Corps was disbanded in 1949.

Cadet Corps in Harbour Playground.

THE JOINT RECTORSHIP

1918 brought a crisis of another kind to the academy. In January a formal motion was presented to the School Board relating to the rector, and on 28th February by six votes to two, Alexander Emslie was dismissed.

William Dick

H.A. Jamieson

Surviving evidence suggests that the basic cause was a clash of personalities. Emslie's behaviour appeared dictatorial to some people. Masters accustomed to their traditional independence resented rectorial supervision. Board members found him obstructive when they were making new staff appointments and exercising their general management of the school. In 1915 he had agreed to undertake additional teaching duties because of wartime difficulties; the Board refused repeated demands for an increase in his salary of £500; he insisted on operating according to the strict terms of his contract as he interpreted it; this position the Board found intolerable. Emslie argued that Board members were motivated by personal animosity, mentioning among others Duncan MacKay, now elected to the Board after his retiral from the academy: 'a source of friction in my predecessor's time as well as mine.' The dismissed rector could claim widespread popular support. A protest meeting filled the Town Hall, and five thousand out of eight thousand electors signed a petition in his favour. Tom Paterson, later a bailie of Ayr, on behalf of the Ayr Labour Club described the Board's action as 'malevolent, oppressive.' All appeals failed and Emslie at the age of 44 went off to find another post in Belfast.

When Emslie was summarily dismissed the two senior masters, William Dick and Hugh Jamieson, were invited to undertake 'in the meantime' the duties of rector in addition to their departmental responsibilities. On previous occasions Robert Taylor and Duncan MacKay had been similarly given interim authority till a new rector was brought in. This time, however, the temporary arrangement became permanent, and confirmed when School Boards were abolished by the Education (Scotland) Act of 1918 and control passed to the new elected Ayrshire Education Authority.

This new body could more effectively extend educational provision. Ayr Burgh School Board had heavy financial burdens, not least of which had been its magnificent provision of a new academy involving initial outlay of £9000 (1880) supplemented by £3000 (1895), £8000 (1907) and over £12000 (1912). The Board had necessarily to maintain high fees which only a limited number of families could afford. The roll of 420 pupils in 1880 actually dropped to 385 by 1900. Thereafter there was an increase to 517 (1910) and 573 (1918). Continued residential development south of Miller Road contributed to the general increase in Ayr's population from 21,000 (1881) to 36,000 (1921) and provided these additional recruits to the academy roll. But the augmented income from fees was all absorbed in providing increased salaries for a necessarily increased staff of 39 by 1918.

The purpose of the 1918 Act was to extend secondary education, and the school leaving age was raised to fourteen. Ayrshire Education Authority was required to provide necessary facilities. Certain elementary schools acquired supplementary classes, some became Higher Grade schools — Newton Academy, Russell Street, and the Grammar School in Ayr, with Prestwick, Troon, and Dalmellington in the vicinity. So did St Margaret's School, which like all other R.C. schools now came under public control as a 'transferred school.' Increased numbers of secondary pupils put pressure on accommodation. A new primary school was built at

Heathfield (1928). This followed an abortive proposal (1925) to provide a new building for the academy's primary department at Barns Park.

Elsewhere in the county, full six year secondary courses were being developed in places like Cumnock, Maybole, and Girvan, so that pupils from these areas no longer had to travel into Ayr. Ayr Academy had become the senior secondary school for the burgh and adjacent areas. In the management of all this redevelopment, Ayrshire Education Authority was supervised by the Scottish Education Department (henceforth no longer 'Scotch') whose headquarters were transferred from Whitehall to Edinburgh. And a national scale of minimum salaries for teachers was instituted.

The academy's clientele was significantly altered. By 1923 fees in secondary classes were reduced to £4 a year and in 1927 were totally abolished. In the primary department pupils continued to pay fees (£4 to £6 per year) and progressed into the intermediate and senior secondary departments where they were joined by others coming in from various local schools at the beginning of the first or fourth years. Between 1918 and 1932 the number winning a group leaving certificate increased from 34 to 48.

A typical pupil of this time was William Ross, son of a railwayman, who came to the academy from Russell Street School in 1923 at the age of 12. After five years' secondary schooling in the academy he went on to graduate at Glasgow and become a teacher. He served in the Second World War, reaching the rank of major. From 1946 till 1979 he was M.P. for Kilmarnock and was Secretary of State for Scotland in two Labour administrations. He was made a life peer with the title of Lord Ross of Marnock.

Lord Ross recalls his schooldays when 'the Heavenly Twins' were rectors. Of his teachers he remembers especially Miss McWilliam who 'must head the list'; 'that grand old man, James McClelland'; Robert McMillan 'who never merited the nickname of Bully'; and 'Daddy Parkyn who when he found anyone who couldn't draw a straight line prophesied for him a place on the town council.' In those days rugby reigned supreme. 'It must have been around 1926-7 when some of us got involved in forming an "illegal" Ayr Academy soccer team. We even got a master to referee for us — Newton Park

CLASSROOM STUDIES ABOUT 1900

was our venue. The venture was short-lived. In one game J.B. Stevenson of Troon (later a well-known golfer) had to have stitches put in his lip. The doctor sent the bill to the school. End of soccer in Ayr Academy.' Many of the contemporaries of Willie Ross did well in their chosen careers, as he remembers. He notes how many from the academy went into various kinds of public service. Before his time there was a boy from the Newton who became Sir Thomas McIlwraith, Prime Minister of Queensland. Sir Andrew Duncan, for some time an assistant teacher here, became a government minister. Locally, Tom Limond became a noted Town Chamberlain of Ayr. Much later in 1955 'Sandy' McMillan the English teacher collaborated with this Thomas Limond and A.L. ('Ross') Taylor, another distinguished former pupil — to produce **Bairnsangs** by 'Sandy Thomas Ross.'

This was the last generation of pupils travelling daily by train from quite distant parts of the county. Some left Muirkirk at six in the morning, changed trains at Auchinleck, and carried candles so they could do their homework en route. Some boisterous pupils from Mauchline used to stick their legs out of the carriage windows on rainy mornings, and with wet feet in school claim seats next to the radiators.

The joint rectorship of Dick and Jamieson operated till they retired simultaneously in 1932. Their administration appears to have been efficient enough, though as can be imagined there were certain complexities. Former pupils recalled that when 'sent to the rector' one could make a discreet choice; and when refused a request by one rector, one could always try the other. They apparently complemented each other. Jamieson when he came as a young man in 1901 had been noted for his stern-ness, but he now had indifferent health. Dick since coming in 1895 had suffered increasing absentmindedness. On one occasion he left his infant son by the bookstall in St Enoch Station, Glasgow, and arrived home in Ayr without him.

Fortunately there was a remarkable continuity in the administration of the various departments. The Art master, J. Herbert Parkyn (1912— 26), was followed by T. Bonar Lyon (1926—38), both noted artists, the former remembered for his eccentricities. The first Science master, Robert McMillan (1896—1926), universally known as 'Bully' because of his bulldog look, retired after forty years teaching in the academy, to be followed by John Begg (1926—45). Ewan Ritchie (1907—1928) was succeeded by William Duff (1928—48) as Manual Instructor in charge of the growing Technical department. The first Infants Mistress, Margaret Buchanan (1895—1924) gave way to Mary G. White (1924—37). The heads of the other departments all served throughout this formative period; James McClelland (1917—42) in Classics; Ada Jaffray (1916—38) in Modern Languages; Jemima Murray (1912—41) in Domestic Science; T.B. Watson (1921—63) and Christina Moodie (1917—37) as instructors in Physical Training. Frederick Ely continued as part-time Music teacher. The English and Mathematics departments were supervised by the rectors. The teacher of Commercial Subjects was James F. Short (1913—24) and the Lady Superintendent was Isabella Riddel (1919 —23); but neither was replaced. Throughout this period Miss Jessie Morgan (1915—45) served as school secretary. As janitor, Adam Loudon (1905—23) was followed by his son, another Adam Loudon (1923—63) familiarly known as 'Ned.' By 1932 the teaching staff included 7 preparatory teachers, 38 secondary teachers, plus two part-time teachers of music, to cope with a roll which had grown from 573 (1918) to 970 (1932).

During this period the various extra-curricular activities which had been earlier introduced became now firmly established. Emslie, protesting in 1918 against his dismissal, had claimed credit for innovations: rugby, cricket, and hockey had been joined by golf, tennis, swimming, and cycling clubs; the Cadet Corps had been instituted; the Literary and Debating Society formed; also a Field Club and a Camera Club; and the magazine had begun regular publication. After some inevitable wartime dislocations all these activities flourished and were augmented. Boxing contests were introduced in 1921; a Girl Guides company began meeting in 1922; badminton is mentioned in 1924. In 1926 silver bowls were donated for the Sports champions, and in the following year the town council made part of the Old Racecourse available for games. Under Frederick Ely's baton, school choirs established a triumphant reputation at the annual Ayrshire Music Festivals, which he had himself instituted in 1912. Annual school concerts were presented from 1925. In 1930 the school was equipped with gramophone and radio, supplementing the lantern slides which had been in use since 1906, thus extending further the horizons of the academic pupils.

The Tuck Shop.

John Bowman, Emeritus Professor of Middle Eastern Studies
in the University of Melbourne, recalled his days as a pupil at
Ayr Academy between 1921 and 1934. 'I can remember the
names of my Primary teachers! Miss Kinghorn, Miss
Buchanan, Miss Crawford, Miss McPhail and Miss Maggie
Morton. These teachers patiently helped me and my class-
mates lay the foundations, sound foundations, for our
future education.' In the Secondary department, he
remembered 'Pussy' McWilliam who could be sardonic, even
caustic, but who imparted a deep appreciation of
Wordsworth and Keats; 'Caesar' McClelland and his
Australian assistant Miss Mary 'Medusa' Anderson; 'Feety'
Anderson who would 'come in, put a problem in algebra on
the blackboard, then sit down and read his newspaper . . . He
informed us that in a few years we would go on to university
and would have to learn there how to educate ourselves.'
Other former pupils have recalled the extra-curricular life of
the school in the late twenties. 'At the intervals we were not
allowed to go further than the tuck shop across the road
but in the Senior Girls Room we picked out two each day to
run the gauntlet to Girdwoods at the end of Cathcart Street
where we bought doughnuts or honey buns — two for one

84

penny — and they were just out of the oven and quite delicious. Occasionally one or two were caught with their huge bag of buns and made to stand in the middle of the hall, as punishment, with their bundle . . . The Literary and Debating Society was very popular, not only for the debates but I suspect because it was the breeding place for many a school romance. Mr Dick and Mr Jamieson were well aware of the situation and we had to tell our parents that the meeting finished at 9 p.m. We were allowed to attend this club without our school uniforms and so there was quite a competition to be as smart as possible. Many of the boys wore the then fashionable plus fours. One of the favourite meetings was the mock parliament. I remember Tom Limond as the Conservative leader and Willie Ross for Labour.'

This period saw the revival of a society for former pupils. As far back as 1888 an old boys' dinner had been held. An association was then formed, mainly of Glasgow businessmen, which by 1907 was known as the Ayr Academy Club. In 1910 there was the first of a series of annual reunions. In 1911 when the suffragettes were active, the question arose of allowing female former pupils to join; a temporary compromise was reached that ladies might be invited as guests of the all-male committee. After the war this club was revived for a few years, and was resuscitated for a third time in 1932.

The president of the Ayr Academy Club in 1924, Sir Alexander Walker, donated new prizes for Science. Two years earlier an Isabella Laurie prize for the best 3rd Year girl pupil had been instituted. Other prizes came from the London Ayrshire Society, the Edinburgh Ayrshire Association, and Ayr Burns Club. A still more important donation to the academy followed in 1931 in a bequest from Major E.M. Innes Taylor: a Raeburn portrait of John Ballantine, who had played so important a role in creating Ayr Academy; plus a miniature and letter from Robert Burns to Ballantine, these later presented on loan to the Burns Cottage Museum.

THE SENIOR SECONDARY SCHOOL

By the Local Government (Scotland) Act of 1929, Ayr County Council greatly increased its powers, taking over control of education from the Ayrshire Education Authority which now passed out of existence. It was the Education Committee of the County Council which acquired responsibility for the management of Ayr Academy and in particular for the appointment of a successor when the joint rectors retired in 1932.

Dr James Ritchie

Their choice was James Ritchie (1932—45) from Forres Academy. A Doctor of Science and a Fellow of the Royal Society of Edinburgh, he was a man of wide interests. He was, said the S.E.D. report of 1934, 'an enlightened and cultured personality.' A former pupil described him as possessing 'the two seemingly contradictory qualities of dignity and energy.' With lively enthusiasm he set about bringing some new-fashioned ideas into the academy.

A standardised school uniform was introduced. Since 1912 when a coat of arms had been acquired, the school badge was worn by boys on their caps and by girls on their sailor hats. Now boys were required to wear maroon blazer and cap with badges, and a maroon and white tie; girls wore a maroon blazer and navy blue tunic with badges, and a hat with maroon and white band. For fee-paying primary pupils this could be insisted upon; with secondary pupils for whom an academic education, though free, was a privilege, the wearing of uniform became the norm. At the same time Dr Ritchie noted in the school logbook: 'Gowns are now being worn by the staff.'

A prefect system was introduced. Back in 1913 this had been tried. Now in 1932 eight boys and eight girls from the senior class were chosen by the rector to lead the 313 preparatory, 466 intermediate, and 221 senior pupils. At the same time, to stimulate competition, both scholastic and athletic, a House system was introduced. The school was divided into five 'Houses' taking the names of Kyle, Carrick, Cunningham from the ancient divisions of Ayrshire, and from local estates, Craigie and Rozelle. Ayr Academy Club presented a House Silver Shield, and Messrs Forbes and Ferguson donated a trophy for the Prep. department.

THE PREFECTS, 1933.
Top: J. Paton, H. Cowan, W. Welsh, J. Wilson.
Centre: R.C. Parker, E. Gilfillan, N.R. Lancey, D. Munro, N. Calderwood, W. Browning.
Bottom: T. McCartney, A. Dunlop, Dr. Ritchie, E.S. Ewen, J. Middleton.

The school song was composed in 1933. The words were by William Dick, the recently-retired rector. The music was by Frederick Ely, who in this year became at last a full-time music master. Miss Elizabeth McIntyre, his assistant, composed an 'Ayr Academy March.' A school orchestra and a four-part choir were formed. Each morning at assembly they performed, with the other pupils singing from the newly-published 'Songs of Praise,' hymns chosen by Dr Ritchie. In 1934 the Academy Song and March were presented on gramophone record.

SCHOOL SONG

"RESPICE, PROSPICE."

Words by
WILLIAM DICK, M. A.

Set to Music by
FREDERIC ELY B. Mus. (Lond.)

school   by the   Ayr___   and the   wind · dri · ven   sand · dunes, Our
Cour · age they   gave___   us, en · dur · ing en · deav___ our. ___
Home · land and   far___   lands___ Young   now no   long · er. ___
Still   may our   thoughts of   thee___   On   to   life's   end · ing. ___

D. C.

Scots ___ youth have   thronged ___   from the first ___   to ___ the   last.
Strong ___ wills   to   brace ___   us in   work ___ and ___ in   play.
Quest · ing ___ glad ___   ven · ture in   air. ___ earth or   sea.
Keep   our ___ feet ___   stead · fast in   hope. ___ love ___ and   truth.

D. C.

fff Maestoso

After v. 2 Flor · u · it   sem · per   Ac · a · de · mi · a l
After v. 4 Flor · e · at   sem · per   Ac · a · de · mi · a l

fff

rall. ___

89

Appropriately all this coincided with the opportunity to celebrate the 700th anniversary of the school in 1933. There was an open-air pageant on the Low Green on Saturday 24th June; a dramatic suite entitled 'The Buik of the Schule of Air' in the Town Hall on 27th and 28th June; and a Celebration Dinner on 29th June. In a special issue of the magazine James Cassels reviewed the history of the academy. More permanent memorials were provided. A commemorative tablet was unveiled in Ayr Auld Kirk. Ayr Academy Club presented a flag pole, supplying later in 1951 an embroidered school flag. They also arranged for a permanent Academy Museum display in the central hall. That hall was itself enhanced by a Rostrum donated by Sir Thomas Oliver, and above it in the scheme of redecoration were inscribed the Biblical words: 'Wisdom is the Principal Thing. Therefore get Wisdom, and with all the Getting get Understanding.' Later, on Thursday 24th May 1934 the academy was honoured by a brief visit of the Prince of Wales, later King Edward VIII.

Visit of The Prince of Wales, 1934.

The school roll of 970 when Dr Ritchie became rector in 1932 remained for a time static. The primary department had to limit admissions because of accommodation; and in the secondary department facilities particularly in science were quite inadequate. Late in 1934 Ayr County Council accepted the need for enlargement. Land behind the school was acquired and on this difficult site the County architect, R.G. Lindsay, designed an extension. Building began in 1936 and the new suite of classrooms and laboratories was almost ready on the outbreak of was in 1939. With the inspiration of Dr Ritchie, the enthusiasm of the architect, and the balance of the First World War Memorial fund, it was possible to transform a proposed lecture room into the Memorial Hall. Into this was incorporated a library, still on a limited scale, but an improvement on the old McCowan Library which was just a collection of books till the Memorial Hall was opened in 1940. Later in 1953 there was a generous donation of £1000 from Sir Douglas McInnes Shaw to equip the proper library it was hoped would eventually be established. A different but equally necessary facility was also improved. The small dining room provided in 1912 was no longer sufficient. As an alternative Lady Jane Hamilton's School in Charlotte Street was converted to provide a new dining hall, opened in 1946.

The Extension, 1936.

The extended accommodation allowed for a temporary increase in wartime numbers. In 1940 for a time the roll was

1223, including 236 evacuees, mostly from Glasgow, but from no fewer than 72 schools altogether. After the end of the war there was more permanent augmentation of numbers as a result of County Council policy.

In the 1930s the core of the academy was still the three hundred preparatory pupils who were admitted on payment of fees and who thereafter passed into the secondary department. Of the seven hundred secondary pupils, around two-thirds were entrants from other local schools. Most came from Ayr itself and few from further away than Dalmellington and Troon (or Prestwick after Troon acquired its own Marr College in 1935). Indeed it was calculated in 1940 that of 1060 pupils, 930 went home from lunch. After the war, County Council policy in line with current fashion in educational theory decreed that all pupils should be taught according to age, ability, and aptitude. This meant that junior secondary schools should cater specially for pupils who intended to end their education at the statutory leaving age, which was raised to fifteen in 1947. All those who wished a full academic secondary course and were deemed intellectually fit for such by county primary promotion tests were directed towards senior secondary schools like Ayr Academy. Incidental to such a policy, fee paying in all Ayrshire schools was abolished in 1947. The primary department of Ayr Academy was finally phased out between 1953 and 1960. Thereafter Ayr Academy became entirely a selective secondary school.

As the magazine boasted: 'The doors of Ayr Academy are wide open to talent.' Thirty five per cent of the children of Ayr and neighbourhood could gain entrance. Of the two hundred admitted annually about a third went on to gain the group leaving certificate. In 1948 Ayr Academy had 64 successful candidates out of Ayrshire's total that year of 271. Two years later the Leaving Certificate was modified — passes in an entire group were no longer necessary for an award. The 'high flyers' still needed the usual range of subject passes, and in 1964 the academy sent 51 entrants to university. Those who could achieve only a few 'highers' now obtained some recognition. And the academy continued its traditional policy of catering for pupils of more limited academic interests. Intensive commercial, domestic, and technical courses were offered. In addition, during the Second World War, pre-apprenticeship courses in building were begun in Ayr and Kilmarnock Academies. Boys throughout the county were eligible and brought in for their special vocational classes, a successful pioneering venture culminating in their transfer to new technical colleges.

The final conversion of Ayr Academy into this selective senior secondary school took place after the sudden and lamented death of Dr Ritchie in 1945. He was followed by J. Douglas Cairns (1945–65) who had already served here effectively some years before as a principal teacher under Dr Ritchie and was particularly suited to succeed him. J.D. Cairns came from Edinburgh with qualifications in English and philosophy. He was inspiring as a teacher not only in the classroom but in the wider field of adult education.

J.D. Cairns

He combined literary with outdoor interests — hill walking, school cruises, and especially rugby — and he cycled daily to school. He continued fit enough to turn out at the Old Racecourse assisting the younger boys at rugby training. On his retiral he was eulogised for his 'humanity, kindness, and friendship.'

Between 1932 and 1965 Dr Ritchie and Mr Cairns were ably supported by an outstanding team of principal teachers. Often, however, they stayed here only a short time before gaining merited further promotion. The English department was in the hands of J.D. Cairns (1932–35), Alastair MacKenzie (1935–40), W.T.H. Inglis (1940–45), Lawrence Holland (1945–47), Alexander MacMillan (1947–53). Mr Inglis left to become Director of Education for Ayrshire and all the others became rectors. From the English department two separate departments emerged. History was developed under Hugh McGhee (1949–53), Adam S. Dobson (1953–59), Robert Y. Corbett (1959–66); Geography under Miss Joy Manson (1949–57) and Ernest H.W. Burt (1957–71). The Classics department had for a long period been run by

James McClelland (1917—42). Known as 'Caesar' to generations of pupils, he had been a pupil from 1891—95, was an authority on the academy's history, and continued riding his bicycle around Ayr till the age of ninety. He was followed by Charles C. Jenkins (1942—53) and Alex. F. Duncan (1953—66). In charge of the Mathematics department was another with a long forty-seven year knowledgeable association with the academy, James Cassels (1916— 38). He was renowned for his mathematical prowess, and as the 'kindliest, happiest, healthiest of mortals' was familiarly known as 'Sunny Jim.' He was succeeded by Thomas D. Murray (1958—72), another of similar pattern.

THE STAFF, 1933 — Back Row: Messrs Duff, A. Wilson, Skinner, Johnstone, W. Inglis, W. Anderson, A.W. Wilson, F. Inglis, Watson, Caldwell. 2nd Row: Messrs Fowler, Cairnie, Nicol, Innes, Stratton, Paterson, Lavery, McInnes. 3rd Row: Messrs Forbes and Crawford, Misses Auchinachie, Macintyre, M. Anderson, Murray, Fawcett, Kemp, MacKay, Mr W.M. Anderson. 4th Row: Mr Loudon, Misses Morgan, MacWilliam, Andrew, Philip, Menzies, Kinghorn, Macphail, Lauchlan, Moodie, Crawford, B. Anderson, Morton. Front Row: Messrs Cairns, Lyon, Begg, Miss Jaffray, Dr. Ritchie, Miss White, Messrs McClelland, Cassels, Ely.

The Modern Languages department was administered by Miss Ada Jaffray (1916—38), described as 'a wonderful person' with wide interests; then Leonard White (1938—50), another rector-to-be; and the gentle and cultured William P. Black (1950—70). In the Art department, T. Bonar Lyon (1926— 38), a noted practitioner, was followed by W. S. Kennedy Smith (1938—72). 'K.S.' not only maintained his department's high standards but commanded the Cadet Corps in the war, produced school operas, led parties to Switzerland, and was in 1965 made the first Depute Rector. In the expanding Science department John Begg (1926—45) was succeeded by David Lavery (1945—67) who developed a separate Physics department, with Biology going to Dr Christine Cant (1949—73) and Chemistry to Robert P. McKell (1963—69).

While the main emphasis of the selective secondary school was on the academic subjects, others enjoyed successful growth. Music flourished after Frederick Ely became a fulltime teacher (1933—37) with his own department; the tradition he established was maintained by Edward Glover (1937—62) and by Miss Muriel Cunningham (1962— 81), a former pupil who returned to spend her entire teaching career here. The Domestic Science department, managed for so long by Miss Jemima Murray (1912—41) then Miss Ethel Reid (1947—47) developed into the Home Economics department under Miss Edith M. Lowdon (1947—67). The Technical department which increased in importance under William Duff (1928—48) gained recognition under James W. Bowman (1948—70). Commercial Subjects were re-introduced into the academy in 1939 under Miss Mollie Alderson who was made a principal teacher (1951—73). Physical Education came to occupy a really important part in school life under the dominating presence of T.B. Watson. An able athlete and something of a martinet, 'T.B.' exasperated some but was revered by many more. He fostered enthusiasm for games, trained champions, and led the Cadet Corps. He came in 1921, went off for a couple years to Dollar, returned as Games Master, was promoted to the status of principal teacher in 1951 and retired in 1963 at the age of seventy. For the instruction of the girls he had the assistance of Miss Christina Moodie (1917—37) who became the County's first P.E. supervisor; then Miss Agnes Brock (1937—46).

While there was still a Prep department, the Infants Mistress was Miss Mary C. White (1924—37) and finally Miss Catherine Downie (1937— 53). There was a most appropriate revival of the post of Lady Superintendent (or Woman Adviser). Miss Marion McWilliam had been a member of the English department since 1918. Not only a 'splendid teacher' but an enthusiast who could produce and costume plays, and prepare dramatic scripts for BBC radio, with her abundant energy she made herself 'the backbone of all school activities.' 'Pussy' as she was known throughout all her 45 years on the staff was the obvious choice as Woman Adviser (1946—62). And several other assistant teachers of the period merit passing mention, former pupils who returned to give good service to their old school and made their own particular mark: John S.G. 'Sammy' Boyd in the Mathematics department (1949—70); Miss Margaret Foulds in Art (1963—80); Miss Elizabeth C. Hutchison, P.E. (1948 —). Others with long service were Frank Inglis in English (1926—64) and Miss Margaret Philp in Art (1927—74). With so much varied talent it is not surprising that under Dr Ritchie and later under Mr Cairns it could be said (in the words of the 1937 S.E.D. report) that 'the corporate life of the school is fully developed.'

Sports flourished, under the spirited direction of T.B. Watson, and with the provision of new facilities at the Old Racecourse pavilion in 1933. After 1936 Games periods became a regular part of the curriculum. Rugby, cricket, and hockey were the most popular team sports, and the outstanding practitioners were awarded 'colours' with caps or distinguishing emblems on their uniforms. Girls now also had netball, and there were devotees still for tennis, badminton, golf, and swimming. Annual boxing contests were organised throughout T.B. Watson's time. Cross-country running was instituted in 1949. There were, in 1936 and 1937, entries for the Gareloch yacht races. Interest in the annual sports was stimulated by the House competitions and the award of additional trophies.

The Literary and Debating Society continued its uninterrupted popularity, adding inter-school debates to its programme. In 1935 a Scientific Society was formed to become another permanent feature of school life. Other societies had changing fortunes, depending as they did on varying popular interests and on the enthusiasms of particular teachers. As uniformed organisations went out of fashion the Cadets disbanded in 1949, after 30 years, as did the Girl Guides in 1955, after 33 years. From 1945 there was for a number of years a Junior Red Cross, and a Barnardo's Helpers' League, sharing in the school's increasing charitable concerns. There was for a time a Smallbore Rifle Club, a Photographic Society, a Model Flying Club, and attempts were made to form clubs for hobbies, political dicussion, recorded music, and even conjuring. More successful were the Scripture Union (1951), Chess Club (1945), Stamp Club (1965), and the Merrick and Jungfrau Clubs for hill-walking (1964).

The Drama Club with the Orchestra and Choirs arranged their own and combined performances. They and many others were brought into major co-operative efforts. There was an 'Elizabethan Night' (1932), 'The Buik of the Schule of Air' (1933) and over 200 pupils and a number of teachers participated with others in the 'Pageant of Ayrshire' at the Dam Park (1934). In 1936 'H.M.S. Pinafore' was presented, the first of a successful series of Gilbert and Sullivan operas, continued annually after the war.

'Iolanthe'

School parties at Christmas time became regular in the thirties, and class or group excursions. A few went with Mr Cairns on schoolboy cruises. In 1951 came a summer trip to France; from 1948 onwards participation in the Annual French-Ayrshire summer schools; and from 1954 a series of holiday excursions to Switzerland. All these events are recorded in the magazine which appeared twice a year until the thirties, latterly annually, and after 1964 under the title 'Prospice' developing along less traditional lines with an increased emphasis on artistic presentation.

The Ayr Academy Club for former pupils was revived in 1932 on its most successful basis. There were men's and women's sections, having separate and joint meetings for lectures, discussions, music and bridge. There were groups for rambling and for dramatic production. A London branch was formed in 1937. A club scarf and blazer were designed. Various donations were made to the school. All this had to be discontinued in the war, but thereafter the Club revived once more, with annual dinners.

A Class Trip to Millport.

Sir Thomas Moore, M.P., shows a school party round Parliament.

Former pupils continued to distinguish themselves. In the academic field there may be noted Sir Andrew Watt Kay, Regius Professor of Anatomy at Glasgow University. On the field of sport, the 1st XV of 1957–58 contained Ian McLaughlan who would become a rugger internationalist, the 'Mighty Mouse' who captained the Scottish side; Mike Denness who would become captain of England's Cricket XI; and Ian Ure who became a soccer internationalist. The same year produced Moira Anderson who won renown as a singer.

AYR ACADEMY 1st XV, 1957-58
Back Row: D.J. Caskie, D.M.S. Taylor, J.B. Houston, J.F. Ure, J.F. McCloy, J.B. Anderson, D. Stobie, D.M. Wardrop, T.P. Maxwell. Middle Row: J.S.G. Dunn, R.N. Bryden, J.D. Cairns, Esq. J.H. Hay, T.B. Watson, Esq. M.H. Denness, D.M. Duncanson. Front Row: I. McLauchian, J.A. Craig, S. Kerr.

PRIZES

Prizes had been introduced in 1787. After 1852 the institution of the Cowan gold medal and the Hamilton silver medals offered a range of major awards. The introduction of the Coats gold medal in 1881 was followed by a century in which further generous gifts extended the array of prizes.

Throughout the 19th century the final day of the school session was Examination Day when the very small number of senior pupils wrote their answers to prescribed questions in the morning and prizes were awarded in the afternoon. After 1874 external examiners assessed towards the end of each session the papers for major awards, but Examination Day continued till Maybin's time. After the First World War, with increased numbers of senior pupils, awards were based on the term examinations and the session ended with an evening Prize Giving ceremony, sometimes in the academy, sometimes in the Town Hall.

Prize Day in Central Hall, June 1941.

Changes took place in the financing of some of the awards. The various bequests managed by the Board of Directors were in 1890 transferred to the Ayr Educational Trust and were vested after 1936 in the new Ayrshire Educational Trust. University bursaries were reorganised, and with the abolition of fees in schools the funds of the McCosh bursaries were diverted to other purposes. The old prize funds produced less than £20 annually — Cowan (£3), Coats (£2),

MacDonald (£8), Grant (£5), Hamilton (£1.10/-). By the end of Ritchie's term, it was no longer possible to award medals, and school funds had to subsidise the provision of book prizes. The range of Hamilton medals was reduced to a single book award. Some prizes were discontinued as funds dried up.

But generous benefactors were always available to provide new awards. Thus, for example, the Academy Club in 1936 instituted annual prizes for the best all-round boy and girl. In the post-war era an entire new series was added to the already extensive range: Baillie John Wood Shields (English), Susan Allan (History), William Kirkland (Mathematics), Dr and Mrs Naftalin (Biology), Thomas Limond (Original Poetry), Parent Teachers Association (Modern Studies), Mrs James Anderson (Home Economics), and a revived Margaret Oliver prize for the same subject. There was a Little bequest (Dux boy), supplemented later by a William Reid prize (Dux girl), as well as a Davidson Trophy (Public Speaking), McLaurin Trust prize (General excellence), Ayr and District Round Table prize (Services to the School) and a Clark Achievement Trophy. When Ayr burgh went out of existence in 1975 the long-established Provost's prize dating back to 1855 was continued as the Dallas prize for Mental Arithmetic.

On the Sports field the Academy Club silver cup for boys and the Marshall Silver Bowl for girls were between 1926 and 1960 supplemented by McMurtrie and staff Rose Bowls for prep. girls and boys. There were added a Young Silver Trophy for physical education and the Beveridge Trophy for sports, Dr John C. Wood Trophy for golf, and further awards for P.E. — the Mrs J.D. Cairns Trophy and a series of T.B. Watson Memorial Medals. There were for a time trophies for boxing and shooting, and in connection with the Cadet Corps.

The major awards remained in the field of scholarship — the Cowan Prize for arts and the Coats Prize for sciences, with all principal teachers assessing achievement over a range of subjects. And the names of these outstanding pupils continued to be recorded on the panels overlooking the central hall.

THE COMPREHENSIVE SCHOOL

When Neil McCorkindale in 1965 came from Rothesay to succeed J.D. Cairns as rector of this selective senior secondary school, there were already indications of impending change.

N. McCorkindale

The burgh of Ayr was continuing its growth. From 37,000 (1931) population grew to 42,000 (1951) and 48,000 (1971). With large scale provision of municipal housing, mainly in the east of the town, and continued private residential expansion to the south, additional schools became necessary. Braehead (1951) was the first of a series of new primary schools. To cope also with the additional numbers following the raising of the school leaving age to fifteen (1947) and later to sixteen (1973) the provision of additional secondary schools also became essential. High Schools were opened at Belmont (1960) and Mainholm (1965). These were designed to take those less-academic pupils who had previously gone to junior secondary schools; and also to cater for some who could attempt the new Ordinary grade of the Scottish Certificate of Education which was introduced in 1961. Ayr Academy continued to take those whom primary promotion tests deemed capable of going beyond the Ordinary to the Higher grade of the S.C.E.

However political opinion was now rejecting the formerly popular concept of selection for secondary education according to ability and aptitude, in favour of comprehensive secondary schools. This, it might be argued, was a return to the traditional Scottish system of omnibus schools. Ayr Academy had in the past taken in all pupils from the town, or at least those whose parents had been able and willing to pay. When plans for reorganisation were made public in

December 1967, the rector, a man of strong opinions who had within a short period already made his mark on the school, denounced the proposals as 'aimed at destroying the academic tradition of Ayr Academy.' He took a leading part in a local campaign against Ayr County Council Education Committee in an attempt to 'save Ayr Academy.' But the scheme went ahead despite protests. Belmont and Mainholm were converted from high schools into six-year academies, on equal status with Ayr Academy, which now became an area secondary school taking in all pupils from a prescribed catchment area — north of the river; Alloway; Annbank and Mossblown; some from Coylton; plus senior pupils for a few years more from Prestwick (until 1971) and Dalmellington (until 1978). The first comprehensive intake of 195 pupils was enrolled in the first year classes in 1968. Controversy rumbled on till the end of 1969, when Neil McCorkindale went off to become rector of Perth Academy.

To replace him, the Education Committee chose as rector William Reid (1969–82). Like his predecessor, he was a mathematician; but unlike most previous rectors he was an Ayrshireman, coming from Dalry and Irvine Royal Academy. Over the next decade Ayr Academy was quietly and smoothly converted into a comprehensive school under Mr Reid's supervision.

William Reid

There were various difficulties to be overcome. One passing complication was the phasing out of selective pupils over the period from 1968 to 1973. Large numbers continued during this period in the senior classes: in 1969 there were 600 candidates for Ordinary and Higher S.C.E. exams plus 73 for Sixth Year Studies. Meanwhile the first year intakes increased to around 260 annually. In 1966 the school roll had been 1097. By 1971 it reached a peak of 1350, and the staff increased to more than ninety. But of the comprehensive pupils, a third left at the statutory leaving age, so that as anticipated, the number of senior pupils eventually declined. In 1973 there were 395 S.C.E. candidates. The roll after its temporary inflation settled down to 1130 by 1972.

The school was overcrowded. Huts had to be erected in the playground. Also in 1969 the two buildings of Newton Academy were made available as an annexe, mainly for practical subjects, involving long walks between classes across the New Brig (or an illicit short-cut over the derelict railway bridge). For physical education, the central hall had most inconveniently to be used. The dining hall in Charlotte Street had to be extended in 1967. Many of the facilities which new schools offered just could not be provided here.

For much of this period there was a teacher shortage (and national teachers' strikes in 1965, 1974 and 1980). But the academy staff coped successfully with their numerous problems. Teachers adjusted their methods appropriately to meet the needs of new types of pupil; developed schemes for mixed-ability junior classes; devised courses for those reluctantly retained after the raising of the school leaving age to sixteen in 1973; introduced alternative syllabuses for S.C.E. examinations; catered for the select few following Sixth Year Studies after the introduction of these examinations in 1967; and continued to volunteer their services for a wide range of extra-curricular activites. With the development of comprehensive education throughout Ayrshire, a number of well-qualified teachers went off to promoted posts in other schools; some of the 'old guard' were due for retiral; to replace them and cope with the increased number of pupils, the school benefitted from the arrival of thirty new members of staff in August 1970, a welcome influx of energetic recruits.

During this difficult transitional period, much depended on the experience and abilities of the principal teachers, and in the case of the larger departments assistant principal teachers were appointed to aid them. While some future historian may think fit to assess them individually and record their idiosyncracies, here it may be sufficient to list them. English: Alex R. Jack (1953–72), Norman Lothian (1972 –   ); History: Dr John Strawhorn (1966–74), David Walton (1974– 82), Miss Aileen Fraser (1982–   ); Geography: Ernest H.W. Burt (1957–71), J. Douglas Penman (1971 –   );   Modern   Studies: R.A.   Hogg   (1974–   );

Mathematics: Thomas D. Murray (1958—72), T. Stuart Good (1972—   ); French: William P. Black (1950—68), Robert Colman (1968—   ); German: Willam P. Black (1968—70), John Reid (1970—81); Russian: John Reid (1958—70), Stewart Hunt (1971 —   ); Italian: Miss Avril Sinton (1975 —   ); Classics: Peter Milne (1967—71), Allan Edwards (1971—   ); Chemistry: Robert P. McKell (1963—68), Arch. Wyllie (1968—69), A.S. Hood (1970—   ); Physics: Mervyn C. Thorburn (1967—71), Bryce Yule (1971—81), John McDonald (1981—   ); Biology: Dr Christine Cant (1949—73), Dr J. Jackson (1973—   ); Art: W.S. Kennedy Smith (1938—72), William Lockhart (1973—80), Alexander Caldwell (1980—   ); Home Economics: Miss Edith Lowdon (1947—67), Miss Janet Wark (1967— 70), Mrs M. McCartney (1970—78), Miss Helen Scott, later Mrs Whiteford (1978—81), Mrs S. Blackwood (1980—   ); Technical Subjects: James W. Bowman (1948—70), Nicol Francis (1970—74), W.F. McLean (1974—   ); Business Studies: Miss M. Alderson (1939— 73), Mrs M.S. Struthers (1973—   ); Religious Education: John A. Bone (1971—   ); Music: Miss Muriel Cunningham (1962—81), Raymond Bramwell (1981 —   ); Physical Education: John R. McClure (1963—77), Peter Connolly (1977—   ); Remedial Education: Mrs Janik (1968—74), Miss I. R. Porter (1975—   ).

As schools became larger, even before the introduction of comprehensive education, a more elaborate administrative structure was introduced by Ayr County Council Education Committee. The rector was given the support of a Depute Rector, W.S. Kennedy Smith (1965—72) followed by Thomas W. Henderson (1972—   ). Assistant Rectors were also appointed in 1971, originally four in number: James A. Naismith (1971—74), Ernest H.W. Burt (1971—74), Mrs Agnes Le Harivel (1971—80) who since 1962 had followed Miss McWilliam as Lady Adviser, Mrs Elizabeth Rennie (1971—   ), Dr John Strawhorn (1974—82), Nicol Francis (1974—   ), David Walton (1982—   ).

In 1968 housemasters were appointed, later renamed Principal Teachers of Guidance, responsible for the welfare of pupils who might otherwise be neglected in a large school population. In Ayr Academy a horizontal division was preferred and Guidance principals (with assistants) became responsible for year groups. Those appointed were Mrs Elizabeth Rennie (1968—71) followed by Miss Marion M.

Gaw (1971–); Robert S. Burns (1968– 82); W.F. McLean (1968–74) then Robert Fulton (1974–); Roy G. Storie (1968–70) then James McHardy (1970–); and D.S. Lennox (1972–) responsible for Careers guidance.

The large teaching staff was supported by a librarian (from 1975); three secretaries; six auxiliaries (following the appointment of a first laboratory technician in 1964); and three janitors.

Despite the major changes involved in the transition to a comprehensive system, and the trends towards standard-isation accelerated when in 1975 Ayr County Council Education Committee handed over responsibility for schools to the new Strathclyde Regional Council, Ayr Academy retained a distinctive identity.

Special buses now arrived daily to transport many of the pupils from and to their homes. Almost all the younger pupils and those staying beyond school leaving age continued to wear blazers. Each school day began with morning assembly in the central hall. The school hours as evolved over many sessions were retained: 8.55 – 9.25; 9.40 – 12.40; 1.55 – 4. Though there were still prefects, there was rather less regimentation.

The academic tradition was maintained, despite earlier fears. So long as there were selective pupils in the senior classes, one could expect achievements like winning the B.B.C. Top of the Form national contest (1966), and gaining the Sunday Times Chess Tournament trophy twice (1970, 1971). But the comprehensive intake produced senior classes which though smaller in numbers were not in any way behind their predecessors in abilities. In most years Ayr Academy featured in the list of successful candidates in the Glasgow University Bursary competition, and in 1978 there were four among the first fifty winners.

While mixed ability classes were introduced into the first and second years, opportunities were provided to stretch the 'high-flyers.' They could begin a second foreign language in their second year, and 'setting' was arranged in English, Mathematics, and French. When 3rd and 4th year courses were selected by parents, the ablest scientists were from 1974 given the opportunity of studying three science subjects in the time normally allotted to two. In the 5th and 6th years the range of subjects was widened, crash courses in subjects like Italian and Russian offered, certain G.C.E. examinations catered for, and Sixth Year studies undertaken. The traditional prize-giving ceremony continued, advanced to the end of May in 1979 to allow an immediate start to a new session in June. And to widen the pupils' cultural horizons, the long-hoped-for library was at last provided: a full-time librarian was appointed in 1975 and in 1978 a large classroom suitably converted.

Simultaneously, more attention was devoted to those pupils with learning difficulties. A Remedial department was formed in 1968. In the 3rd and 4th years, after experiment-ation here as elsewhere with vocational classes for those leaving at the statutory leaving age, segregated classes were abandoned in favour of an integrated scheme, so that pupils might aim for as many or as few certificate subjects as was considered reasonable. In 1980 ninety per cent of the pupils sat from one to eight S.C.E. examinations, and two out of three presentations resulted in a pass. Among various non-certificate classes provided, a Record of Personal Achievement scheme was introduced. Until it was phased out throughout Strathclyde in 1982, corporal punishment was retained only for such offences as bullying and persistent disobedience.

Modern aids were utilised. The first tape recorder was acquired in 1958, and a first television set in 1968. And two sample instances of innovation: after 1980 all 1st and 2nd year pupils (boys and girls) were taught Technical Subjects and Home Economics; and for all 4th year pupils a week outside school in Work Experience was arranged.

In sports the traditional emphasis on rugby and hockey was sustained. But the scope was widened. Soccer at long last returned to the academy. Since the 1920s it had been disapproved of, and indeed an attempt by the Education Committee officially to insist on its introduction in 1950 proved unsuccessful. Now in contests with other schools, awards were gained for rugby; hockey; soccer; swimming, for which there was a new enthusiasm; and volleyball, which was played by both sexes. To cater for the wider range of interests, in 1973 a new type of Sports Day replaced the traditional series of athletic events, and provided for contests not only in racing but five-a-side soccer, volleyball, archery, golf, tennis, swimming, badminton, and table tennis, all at different venues on one afternoon.

Bus travel to and from school was one factor which limited the appeal not only of sports but of other extra-mural activities. Fund-raising provided a mini-bus in 1976, suitable for the transport of a team or other small group outing, which helped. However, some long-established societies survived: like the Literary and Debating Society, with its annual Burns Supper, the Scripture Union, the Stamp Club, the Chess Club; other groups like the Scientific Society and the hillwalking club continued on a more limited basis; a new Ornithological society was formed; there were various ventures in folk music; choirs and dramatic groups still made successful appearances at festivals; and every other year major musical or dramatic performances were staged. School parties at Christmastide — and now other times — were popular as ever. There were outings in term time to theatres and outdoor centres, and holiday trips to France, Switzerland, Italy and Russia.

One tradition was not only continued but rewardingly enhanced. Community service was noticeably expanded, and charitable efforts sponsored, sometimes on the initiative of groups of pupils. Visits to hospitals and aid to old folk were undertaken. In most sessions there was some major commitment. In 1977 — 78 equipment to the value of £4000 was provided for Seafield Children's Hospital. In 1980 — 81 to mark the Year of the Disabled £2000 was collected for a swim-lift at Ayr Baths. In the various fund-raising activities support was forthcoming from the continuing Former Pupils Club, and the Parent Teachers Association which had been formed in 1967.

But for all the achievements during the rectorship of William Reid, after he retired in 1982 a critical situation faced his successor — William Ballantyne, another north Ayrshireman, from Ardrossan and Garnock Academy, and a scientist.

Because of the Academy's cramped site near the town centre, and the limitations of an ageing building, there had been talk in the seventies of moving Ayr Academy to a new site. In fact the new Kyle Academy opened in 1979 was constructed not as a replacement but as supplementary provision at a time

William Ballantyne

when secondary school rolls were temporarily high. This reduced Ayr Academy's first-year intake from 260 to 180 — a welcome reduction in overcrowding. But a period with a generally-reduced birth rate was now ushering in a spell when the number of secondary pupils would decline. By 1982 the first-year intake at Ayr Academy was nearly half what it had been a decade before; the school roll was dropping below one thousand and seemed destined for continued decline. At this time came the 750th anniversary. Pessimists could envisage the possibility of eventual closure. Optimists could hope that the new young rector could summon the vision of a John Mair and the energy of a Dr Memes to carry forward the academy into another chapter of history. For certainly, as probably the oldest continuing school in Scotland, Ayr Academy can look back over the centuries of its existence with justified pride.

RESPICE — PROSPICE

MASTERS OF THE SCHULE OF AIR AND (from 1796) RECTORS OF AYR ACADEMY.

1233	Allan	1676	James Dickie
—		1680	William Rankin
1502	Andrew McCormyll	1708	James Ferguson
1516	John McKineis	1746	John Mair
1519	Gavin Ros	1761	Alexander Paterson
1541	Patrick Anderson	1768	Arthur Oughterson
1547	Neil Orr	1771	John Inglis
1550	William Nehary	1772	David Tennant
1554	John Buchan	1796	William Meikleham
1559	John Or	1799	Thomas Jackson
1572	Ninian Young	1809	David Ballingal
1595	William Murray	1826	John Memes
1595	Archibald Dunsmuire	1844	Robert McMillan
1597	William Wallace	1844	William Hunter
1605	Alexander Dunsmuire	1862	James MacDonald
1612	John Bonar	1883	William Maybin
1638	William Smyth	1910	Alexander Emslie
1642	William Wallace	1918	William Dick and
1643	John Hamilton		Hugh Jamieson
1649	George Paterson	1932	James Ritchie
1657	Matthew Graham	1945	J. Douglas Cairns
1664	James Fleming	1965	Neil McCorkindale
1666	William Wallace	1969	William Reid
1675	David Skeoch	1982	William Ballantyne

SOURCES OF INFORMATION

1. In Archivist's Department, Regional Office, County Buildings, Ayr:
   Ayr Academy Directors' Minutes 1794—1883.
   Ayr Burgh School Board Minutes 1873—1918.
   Ayrshire Education Authority Minutes 1918—1930.
   Ayr County Council Education Committee Minutes 1931—1975.

2. In Ayr Academy:
   School Log Books, since 1933.
   File of Documents, arranged by years since 1794, including subscription lists, correspondence, accounts, draft minutes, reports, prospectuses.
   Miscellaneous items including for various periods fee books, examination registers, attendance returns, medals, prize books, photographs, samples of pupils' work, school magazines.

3. Printed Books, arranged chronologically:
   James Paterson, **History of the County of Ayr,** Vol. 1, 1847 and 1863 editions.
   James Grant, **History of the Burgh Schools of Scotland,** 1876, with material from Ayr Burgh records supplied by D. Murray Lyon.
   Jane Campbell, ed. **Air Academy and Burgh School,** 1895 — the 'Bazaar Book' including a historical survey by David Patrick.
   J.H. Pagan, **Annals of Ayr 1590—1692,** 1897.
   D.M. Lyon, **Ayr in the Olden Times,** 1928.
   J. Cassels, 'Historical Sketch of Ayr Academy' in **Academy Magazine,** 1933.
   A. Mackenzie, **William Adair and his Kirk 1639—1684,** 1933.
   A. Mackenzie, **An Ancient Church: St John the Baptist of Ayr,** 1935.
   G.S. Pryde, ed. **Ayr Burgh Accounts 1534—1624,** 1937.
   James McClelland, chapter on 'Schools' in **The Royal Burgh of Ayr,** ed. A.I. Dunlop, 1953.
   J.J. Fowler, 'The Presbytery of Ayr: Schools and School Masters' in **Ayrshire Collections,** Vol. 6, 1961.
   W. Boyd, **Education in Ayrshire Through Seven Centuries,** 1961, contains a list of official reports.
   J. McGloin, 'The Abbé Nicolas' in **Innes Review,** 1963.
   A.L. Taylor, 'The Grammar School of Ayr 1746—1796' in **Ayrshire Collections,** Vol. 7, 1966.
   W. Dodd, 'Ayr, a Study of Urban Growth' in **Ayrshire Collections,** Vol. 10, 1972. We acknowledge the use of several of Mr Dodd's plans as illustrations.

RECTOR — Mr William Ballantyne; DEPUTY RECTOR — Mr Thomas Henderson; ASSISTANT RECT
McHardy, Mr D. S. Lennox; ENGLISH-Mr Lothian, Mr Findlay, Mr Mackay, Mrs Fraser, Mr DeBlieck, M
Baillie, Mr McCrorie; MODERN STUDIES-Mr Hogg; MATHEMATICS-Mr Good, Miss Henderson, Mrs
Colman, Mrs Anthony, Miss McKay, Mr McHardy, Mr Henderson; FRENCH ASSISTANT-Mlle Mallin;
McDonald, Dr Spence, Mr Kirkham, Mr Todd; BIOLOGY-Dr Jackson, Miss Gaw, Miss McKell, Mr McVitti
Miss Marshall; HOME ECONOMICS-Mrs Blackwood, Mrs Christie, Mrs Primrose, Mrs McGarry; BUSINE
McKee; PHYSICAL EDUCATION-Mr Connolly, Mr Syme, Miss Hutchison, Mrs McFarlane; RELIGIOUS I
Richmond; JANITORS-Mr Wilson, Mr Morrison, Mr Hendren; SENIOR TECHNICIAN-Mr Holmes; SCIE
Reid; FIRST YEAR-Gordon Baird, Adam Barber, Colin Bennett, Kevin Blair, Gary Bruce, John Coplan
Hainey, Caroline Alexander, Carol Armstrong, Karen Barr, Janet Bryson, Sharon Craig, Allison Dalton, All
Sharon McWhirter, Wendy Speirs, Susan Thomson, Jacqueline Toner. Gordon Bryce, George Campbell,
Jason Kerr, Colin Logan, Craig Murray, Colin Purdie, Sarah Ballantyne, Jennifer Brown, Marie-Ann Cam
Sharon Kennedy, Fiona McCarthy, Pamela McCartney, Elizabeth McClung, Alison McPherson, Barbara I
McGinlay, Gary McIntyre, Ian McKenzie, Peter McMahon, Robert Montgomery, William Mossie, Kevin R
Elaine Harrigan, Sharon Hogg, Gaynor Johnstone, Lorraine Kelso, Karen McCubbin, Yvonne McInnes, I
McCall, Ian McNellie, George McWhinnie, Brian Macey-Lillie, Robin Marshall, Scott Morrison, Robert M
Tracey Hughes, Elizabeth Kelly, Jacqueline Kiltie, Susan Neil, Morna McLelland, Sharon McWilliam, C
Williamson, Ingrid Wilson. Allan Chapman, Archie Harkness, John Osborne, Darren Ross, Steven Russel
Whyte, Ian Wilson, Alison Doolan, Ann McCoull, Valerie McKirdy, Julie McLean, Eunice Rae, Sharon I
Trousdale, Dawn Windley, Suzanne Livingston, Sarah Campbell; SECOND YEAR-Andrew Adams, Stuar
Boyle, Alan Dunlop, Colin Hamilton, Thomas Howat, Jason Hunter, Todd Lynch, Derek John Summers,
Hazel Dunn, Emma Lawrence, May Littlejohn, Paula Nimmo, Lorraine Sharp, Lesley Sweden, Patricia "
Gordon Howie, Alex McCormick, Paul McLelland, David Miller, Mark Murphy, Angus Paul, Ian Ramage,
Alison Fullarton, Shirley Holland, Shelley Houston, Fiona Howie, Dawn Lawson, Fiona Love, Andrea I
David Jones, Brian Logan, Colin Qua, Andrew Robertson, John Shearer, Brian Skivington, Scott Summer
Dudgeon, Sharon O'Pray, Susanne Paterson, Petra Robertson, Joanne Scott, Maura Shearer, Nicola Sing
Gilchrist, Robert Hogg, Walter Hunter, Scott Kirkpatrick, Ian McClune, William McCutcheon, Neil Olive
Debbie Buchanan, Carol-Ann Christie, Catherine Connor, Jacqueline Dalrymple, Elizabeth Dempster, Eliz
Andrew Bryden, David Chan, Richard Hodge, Alex McKelvie, Stephen Mackie, William Milby, William I
Smith, James Smith, Douglas Wark, Nicola Arbuckle, Lai-Ling Koon, Sandra McCubbin, Nicola McGreg
Brown, David Eccles, Thomas Green, Kevin Hainey, Euan Halket, David Johnstone Graham Johnstone, D
Craig Smith, Leigh Gibson, Margaret Brannan, Dawn Bratchie, Karen Campbell, Natasha Christie, Chery
Yates; THIRD YEAR-Andrew Allison, Stuart Allison, Garry Balfour, Mark Barber, John Black, George
Robert Smillie, Matthew Smith, Ross Taylor, Andrew Wood, Marie Adair, Janet Aitken, Arlene Allan, Li
Sloan, Helen Stewart, Pauline Troup. Billy Blane, Philip Clarke, Bert Cowley, Paul Dalrymple, Steven Gle
Alistair Ross, Samuel Ruddock, Finlay Scott, Jonathan Stewart, Philip Street, Andrea Armstrong, Yvor
McFarlane, Sharon McMaster, Jane Shilling, Pauleen Young. Willian Bryden, Mark Cowley, Scott Dunlo
Ghyll McCallum, Richard MacKenzie, Kenneth McLeod, Richard Munro, David Rennie, Mark Sproat, A
McKilligan, Donna McPhee, Fiona Munn, Julieann Robertson, Elaine Wilson. John Gemmell, Derek Gru
Alistair McHarg, David McTaggart, Andrew Malcolm, Stephen Morrison, John Porte, Angela Brown, Tina
Sloan, Grazyna Swierez, Iris Watson. Colin Clark, Colin Davidson, Alex Dunlop, Alexander Jackson,
McLellan, Russell Phillips, Robin Scott, Iain Smith, Robert Walker, Shaun Watson, Nicola Corbett, Joa
Lesley Martin, Linda Monaghan, Diane Porte, Marlene Robb, Gillian Savill, Gayle Simpson, Helen Wint
William McClelland, Raymond Noble, Stephen Noble, David Proudfoot, Murray Stevenson, Alex White
Lynne Powell, Valerie Reid, Isobel Robertson, Christine Smith, Jessica Skilling, Christine Traill, Helen Y
Robert Murdoch, George Paschke, Thomas Paterson, Graeme Rennie, Stuart Taylor, Iain Thursby, Gary
Paula Currie, Rae Duffy, Janet Dunlop, Elizabeth Mair, Janice O'Neil, Amanda Scott, Margaret Thom
William Cree, Simon Davidson, Christopher Holdsworth, Gordon Kerr, Gareth Kirkwood, Colin McA
Margaret Boyle, Alison Ewan, Gillian Forwell, Margaret Ingram, Diane Kerr, Amanda King, Margaret M
Young. Paul Boyd, Stephen Cole, James Cowley, Neil Fletcher, George Gotch, Kevin Hogg, William La
Seaton, Thomas Toner, Joan Aitken, Diane Anderson, Lousie Atkinson, Shona H Black, Paula Dunle
Montgomery, Margaret Morton, Sharon Pride, Eleanor Quinn, Gillian Ruddock. Robert Brodie, Lindsay
Kevin Logan, Kevin Scobie, Cameron Taylor, Scott Thomson, William Thomson, Douglas Wilson, Rac
Marion Murdoch, Pamela Murray, Jane Newbold, Kirsty Ramage, Alison Sey, Linda Smillie, Karen Tuto
McDougall, Angus McKenzie, James McLachlan, Alistair Murdoch, Thomas Potts, Shayne Scott, Robin
Elizabeth Coyle, Yvonne Harrigan, Jacqueline Holland, Gail Lawson, Pamela Livingston, Rebecca Ridli
James Cairns, Scott Davies, Peter Dickie, Stephen Donnelly, Duncan George, George Hepburn, Alexander
Tracy Anderson, Jackie Brambles, Julia Brown, Karen Conn, Alison Hall, Rose Hill, Vickie Lapsley, Z
Dunlop, John Findlay, Ian Hamilton, John Jamieson, Gregor Johnston, Brain McGregor, Willam Rob
Lorraine Brown, Lynne Cochrane, Angela Dunlop, Christine Farrell, Patricia Graham, Fiona Kean, M
Thomson. William Brown, Campbell Holland, Andrew Ireland, Paul Kennedy, John Law, Scott McCros
Karen Courtney, Rhona Cowe, Lesley Dawson, Kirstie Eccles, Julia Grant, Julie McCubbin, Jilian Marsl
Smith, Sharon Steven, Michelle Tierney, Rosanne Wilson; FIFTH YEAR-Douglas Eastaugh, Eric Edwar
Lockie, Simon McCormick, Michael McHarg, Kenneth McKay, Martin Ramsay, Grant Rillie, Stewart W
Danks, Kathryn Gill, Pamela McBride, Margaret McLeod, Linda Proudfoot, Christine Savill, Ingrid Smil
Fraser Brown, J Bruce Bunten, Michael Cowley, Michael Daly, James Dinsdale, John Donald, Kenneth
Berry, Gilllian Boyd, Jacqueline Bryden, Ellis Devlin, Marelli Feggans, Myra Jones, Karen McKay, Se
Glencorse, Michael Hall, Stephen Holland, Derek Ireland, Craig Kennedy, David Kennedy, Timothy Lawi
David Scobie, Ian Sweden, Alan Wilson, Charles Winton, Lynn Aitken, Elizabeth Allison, Gillian And
Lorraine Davidson, Angela Ferguson, Anne Gourlay. Jonathan Anson, Andrew Bryson, David Clark, C
Alistair Hood, Ian Jess, Peter Johnston, Roy Lockhart, Gordon McCracken, Linda Agnew, Audrey Holla
Karen McLean, Audrey Macgee, Katriona Marshall, Dawn Ritchie. Jamie Kirkland, Alan McDonald, Ian
Nicholas Watkins, Adrian Waterton, Donald Welsh, Scott Williams, McKenzie Wilson, David Yates, Harry
Alison Stewart, Kirsteen Straiton, Jane Taylor; SIXTH YEAR-Andrew Carr, David Connell, Thomas Co
Lawrence, Neil McAdam, Alan Poole, Blaney Quinn, John Shields, James Stevenson, Robert Stuart, Jane
Glynis Neagle, Lindsay Phillips, Hazel Smart, Lorna Watson, Alison Young. Michael Andreason, David
Alan Porte, Sean Rowe, Matthew Short, Derek Simpson, Forbes Simpson, Alan Smith, Stuart Welch
McLelland, Helen Oates, Jacqueline Pirie, Moira Shaw, Sara Short, Jayne Street. David Byars, Alastair I
Nixon, Donald Paterson, Steven Pendrill, Andrew Wright, Carolyn Davie, Jennifer Dawes, Dawn Herri
Lorraine Quigley, Morag Ramage, Fiona Robertson, Shirley-Anne White.

750 years of
A Scottish School
AYR ACADEMY 1233-1983

© Dr. John Strawhorn

First Published in 1983
by
Alloway Publishing Ltd.,
39 Sandgate, Ayr.

Printed in Scotland
by
Walker & Connell Ltd.,
Hastings Square, Darvel,
Ayrshire.

ISBN 0 907526 10 1

CONDITIONS OF SALE